for Howard & Shirley Lamar
in remembrance of the great week
in Santa Fe, September, 2007
Tom & Nancy Creighton

Dorothy Scarritt McKibbin

GATEKEEPER TO LOS ALAMOS

by Nancy Cook Steeper

(our baby-sitter when
she was a high schooler
in Denver)

Los Alamos Historical Society
Los Alamos, New Mexico
2003

Library of Congress Cataloging-in-Progress Data

Gatekeeper to Los Alamos : Dororthy Scarritt McKibbin / by Nancy Cook Steeper.

p. cm.

Includes bibliographical reference and index.
ISBN 0-941232-30-1 (pbk. : alk. paper)

1. McKibbin, Dorothy Scarritt. 1897-1985. 2. Los Alamos (N.M.)--Biography. 3. Secretaries--New Mexico--Los Alamos--Biography. 4. Los Alamos Scientific Laboratory--Biography. 5. Manhattan Project (U.S.)--Biography. 6. Scientists--New Mexico--Los Alamos--History--20th Century. 7. Los Alamos (N.M.)--Social life and customs--20th Century. I. Title: Dorothy Scarritt McKibbin, Gatekeeper to Los Alamos. II. Title

F804.L6S74 2003
978.9'58052'092--dc21
[B]

2003045201

Photo credits: Photographs are from the McKibbin Family Papers unless otherwise noted.

Cover sketch, courtesy of Francoise Ulam, was made by the Austrian physicist Otto Frisch in 1950.

Los Alamos Historical Society
P.O. Box 43
Los Alamos, New Mexico 87544

Printed in the United States of America

For Kevin,
as Dorothy meant it to be

TABLE OF CONTENTS

INTRODUCTION

A bronze plaque in the courtyard of an ancient Spanish hacienda at 109 East Palace Avenue, Santa Fe, New Mexico, reads:

> 1943 SANTA FE OFFICE 1963
> LOS ALAMOS SCIENTIFIC LABORATORY
> UNIVERSITY OF CALIFORNIA
> All the men and women who made the first atomic bomb passed through this portal to the secret mission at Los Alamos. Their creation in 27 months of the weapons that ended World War II was one of the greatest scientific achievements of all time.

On March 27, 1943, Dorothy Scarritt McKibbin, a 45-year-old woman of great warmth, patience, and optimism, became the first permanent employee of that Santa Fe office and the gatekeeper of that venerable doorway.

Two days before Dorothy began her work at 109, she was crossing Palace Avenue in the center of Santa Fe. In the middle of the street, she met a man named Joe Stevenson. She and Joe and his wife, Adele, had been friends for many years. The Stevensons had recently returned to town after a long period away. Rumor was that they were in California, taking some kind of training course related to the war.

With traffic moving around them in both directions, Joe Stevenson said to Dorothy, "How would you like to have a job as a secretary?"

"Well, I don't know," Dorothy replied. "Can you tell me anything about it?"

"Don't you know what a secretary does?" Joe asked.

"Not always," she responded.

He implied that the project was too secret to explain in any detail and gave her twenty-four hours to think it over. In the course of the evening, she called her friends and asked, "Have you heard of any new enterprise coming to town that needs a secretary?" No, they had heard of nothing.

The following day Dorothy went to the lobby of La Fonda, the hotel at the end of the Santa Fe Trail and a central meeting place for Santa Fe residents and visitors. She came upon Joe Stevenson who was talking with a man she thought might be from California. Her criteria? He had on a brown silk gabardine suit; the coat matched the pants. He was wearing a white shirt, necktie, and dress shoes, unusual attire seldom seen in Santa Fe. Joe introduced the man as Duane Muncy who did indeed turn out to be from California.

The three were chatting casually when Dorothy noticed a man walking toward them. He was wearing a trench coat and a porkpie hat and carrying a pipe. She described him as "tall and slender, graceful in every movement,"[1] and noted that he walked on the balls of his feet as though they were barely touching the ground. The newcomer stopped to say hello to the men, and they introduced him to Dorothy. She said, "Hello," but did not catch his name. If she had, it would have meant nothing to her.

After he turned to leave but was no more than six feet away, she said to Joe Stevenson and Duane Muncy, "I will take the job." Something about the way Joe and this man spoke to each other suggested to Dorothy that he was connected with the job being offered.

Many years later Dorothy would write:

> I thought to be associated with that person, whoever he was, would be simply great! I never met a person with a magnetism that hit you so fast and so completely as his did. I didn't know what he did. I thought maybe if he were digging trenches to put in a new road, I would love to do that, or if he were soliciting ads for a magazine or something, I would love to do that. I just wanted to be allied and have something to do with a person of such vitality and radiant force. That was for me.[2]

That man was J. Robert Oppenheimer, scientific director of the Manhattan Project, the top secret mission to build an atomic bomb.

By succumbing to his charm, Dorothy Scarritt McKibbin propelled herself into one of the watershed events of the 20th century. All her life, Dorothy had been a risk-taker. Now she simply could not resist this opportunity to be affiliated with a clandestine operation. Long afterward, she realized that Oppenheimer, who had joined them so casually, had already studied a full dossier on her and had come to La Fonda for the express purpose of meeting her. Without words, in those few moments, he had given his approval for her employment.

The job as "gatekeeper to Los Alamos," which Dorothy accepted so swiftly after her brief encounter with Oppenheimer, was beyond any future she could have imagined for herself, growing up in one of the pioneer families of Kansas City, Missouri, in the early 1900s.

Alexander Lowry, Los Alamos Scientific Laboratory

Dorothy McKibbin in her office at 109 East Palace Avenue in 1963

Part One
EMERGENCE OF THE POWER GIRL

Chapter 1

ROOTS IN KANSAS CITY

Dorothy Ann Scarritt was born on December 12, 1897. Her Scarritt ancestors came from western Scotland in the last decade of the 1600s, settling first in the Connecticut Colony and later in the Lyman, New Hampshire, area. In 1820 family members traveled west by covered wagon and canal boat to Illinois, where her grandfather Nathan Scarritt was born. He left home at age 16 to attend a nearby college and become a teacher. With $10 in his pocket, Nathan moved to Fayette County, Missouri, in 1845. There he founded Howard High School, subsequently renamed Central College (for men), and Howard Female College. Later, Nathan became a minister in the Methodist Episcopal Church. In 1850 he married Martha Matilda Chick, the daughter of William Miles Chick, who had migrated west from Virginia in 1822. Chick built a warehouse at Westport Landing, a steamboat wharf on the Missouri River where the Santa Fe trade and Rocky Mountain fur trade exchanged goods with merchants from the east. He became a prosperous businessman, landowner, and the first postmaster of Kansas City, Missouri.

Over the next twenty-four years, Nathan and Martha Matilda

raised a family of nine children, five boys and four girls. Three of their children died before the age of 20. In 1854 Reverend Scarritt began to carry out his life plan—to preach the gospel and do missionary work among the Indians. He made close friendships with them, and throughout his life tribal chieftains treated him with respect. For the next eight years, with the exception of one year in which he served as president of Central College, he traveled extensively all over Kansas, preaching, making pastoral visits, and organizing churches. He also was director of education at the Shawnee Mission and Manual Training School.

Through judicious real estate investment and property improvement, Nathan Scarritt became a millionaire. During the Civil War he purchased a forty-acre parcel of land, three miles east of Kansas City. He gave parcels of the land to each of his six adult children. In the late 1880s they erected palatial homes that set the architectural and social style for the northeast section of Kansas City. He also served as pastor to five churches and was a major benefactor to the Melrose Methodist Church and a training school for missionaries. When he died in 1890, he was reputed to be the largest landowner in Kansas City.

William Chick Scarritt, Dorothy's father, was the fifth child born to Nathan and Martha Matilda Scarritt. After attending Kansas City public schools, he graduated from Central College in 1881 and from Boston University Law School in 1883. He was admitted to the bar in Missouri and the following year began practicing law with his older brother, Judge Edward Lucky Scarritt.

On July 10, 1884, William married Frances Virginia Davis, a graduate of Howard Payne College. The two met when they were students in Fayette. She was the youngest of thirteen children in another family of Missouri pioneers. Her parents, Temple and Virginia Davis, had migrated west from Virginia and Kentucky and settled near Hannibal, Missouri.

William and Frances Scarritt had five children, two boys and three girls, born between 1886 and 1901. After his first son was born,

Mr. Scarritt commissioned John Wellborn Root, a renowned Chicago architect, to build the mansion in which the Scarritt family was raised. The ornate brownstone and brick residence was constructed in the popular American revival style adapted from the French Renaissance chateaux of the late 15th and early 16th centuries. Twenty-seven first cousins lived in similar houses nearby.

Dorothy Ann was their fourth child and second daughter. William Hendrix (Bill), their first child, was eleven years older than Dorothy. Her constant childhood companions were her sister Frances, six years older than she, and her brother Arthur Davis (A.D.), two and a half years older. Dorothy and A.D. were inseparable as children and devoted to each other throughout their lives. Virginia, the Scarritts' fifth child, died of a respiratory disease in 1907.

A corporate lawyer, William C. Scarritt was a leader in the civic

The W.C. Scarritt home at 3240 Norledge Avenue, Kansas City, Missouri

Dorothy, 8 months old

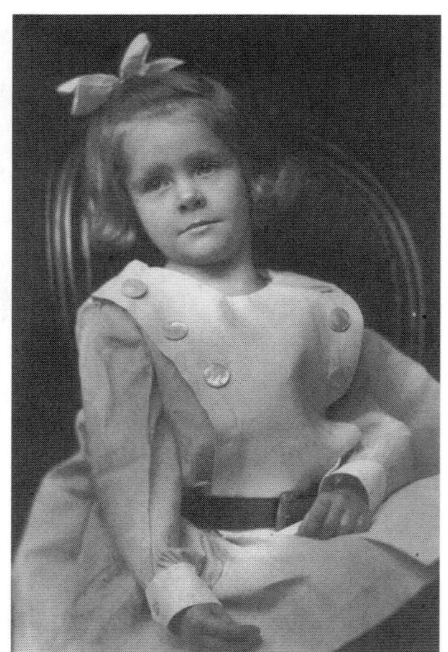

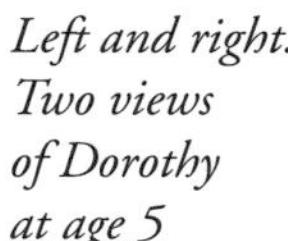

Left and right: Two views of Dorothy at age 5

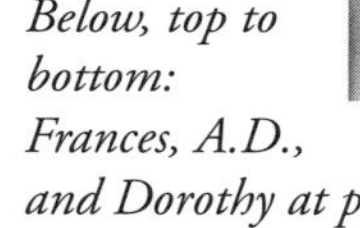

Below, top to bottom: Frances, A.D., and Dorothy at play

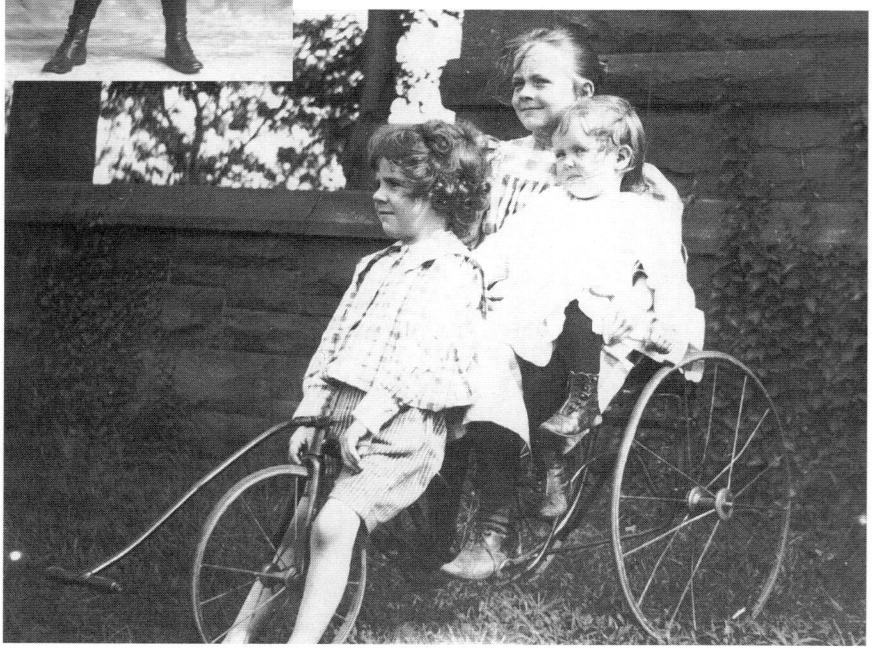

and financial life of Kansas City. He served as police commissioner in 1896-97 and president of the Board of Park Commissioners in 1922. An active Democrat, he was instrumental in shaping Missouri state party politics in the early 20th century. Continuing the family tradition of support for Central College, Dorothy's father provided leadership to the school for more than forty years. The Scarritts were loyal and influential members of the Melrose Methodist Episcopal Church, South, founded by Nathan Scarritt.

Dorothy' s mother, Frances Scarritt

Dorothy's mother was a charter member of the Melrose Fortnightly Club, a social group in Kansas City's northeast district. She was a leader in the YWCA, a member of the Kansas City Rose Garden Association, and a strong supporter of the Kansas City Art Institute. Although public-spirited like her husband, she did not share his political beliefs. One of her granddaughters noted that her red-haired grandmother "fought the Confederate War all her life."[1]

The Scarritts valued education and used their considerable financial resources to provide the best available schooling for their children. In 1908 Bill Scarritt graduated from Williams College in Williamstown, Massachusetts. A.D. graduated from Princeton University ten years later and in 1921 from the University of Kansas City Law School.

Dorothy's formal education began at the Barstow School, a small private day school and the first permanent independent school in the Kansas City area. It was founded in 1884 by a group of prominent civic leaders who were dissatisfied with the quality of public education. Boys attended in the primary grades through junior high when many left to attend male eastern college preparatory schools like Groton, Middlesex, and Phillips Andover. The high school was exclusively for girls, and its curriculum closely followed college entrance requirements for selective eastern women's colleges.

In its early years, Barstow was led by two young graduates of the Class of 1883 at Wellesley College: Miss Ada Brann from Westfield, Massachusetts, and Miss Mary Louise Barstow from Gardiner, Maine. Miss Brann retired in 1899, and the school became "Miss Barstow's School." Miss Barstow was herself a model for the kind of success a women's college graduate might achieve. Her school offered preparation for a number of those distinguished institutions.

Dorothy was one of fourteen young women who graduated in 1915. Her strong academic background included four years each of English, mathematics, Latin, modern languages, and elective courses in history and science. She was editor-in-chief of the school literary magazine, a four-year member of the school drama group, and a forward on the basketball team. She had the potential to be a leader and was clearly a young woman ready to test her talents in a larger, more complex world, thanks to the support of her family and her Barstow training.

Chapter 2

SETTING OUT INTO THE WORLD

In the fall of 1915, Dorothy entered Smith College in Northampton, Massachusetts, one hundred miles west of Boston. Neighboring colleges were Amherst for men and Mount Holyoke, another college for women. Smith was founded in 1871 by Miss Sophia Smith of Hatfield, Massachusetts, who provided the funding for "the establishment and maintenance of an institution for the higher education of young women, with the design to furnish them means and facilities for education equal to those which are afforded in our colleges for young men."[1] With an enrollment of 2,400 students at the time Dorothy entered, Smith was the largest college for women in the United States. Two-thirds of Dorothy's classmates entered Smith from public high schools all across the country; one-third came from private schools. By attending Smith, she had chosen an intellectual and social atmosphere that would broaden her friendships, enlarge her cultural interests, and enrich her life for six decades.

The liberal arts curriculum was organized around a set of core requirements in the first two years which assured that "the foundations are laid for broad and liberal culture for intelligent choice of the major subject to be pursued in the two upper years."[2] In her freshman and sophomore years, Dorothy studied Latin, French, mathematics, physics, English, and history. She was drawn to the latter two subjects as possible majors and vacillated between them. In her third year, she was an English major, but ultimately graduated as a history major. For elective subjects in her last two years, she chose "General History of Art," "General History of Music and Musicians," a philosophy course in logic, an introductory course in psychology, and two sociology courses—"Methods of Social Research" and "Economic Aspects of War."

Dorothy's leadership qualities were recognized immediately. A person of charm and enthusiasm, she was elected president of her class of 577 students in the fall of her freshman year. Coming from a school as small as Barstow, with students from similar backgrounds in the tight social order of Kansas City, Dorothy's early success in an elected position created the impression that she was a "power girl." That perception suited her well. Dorothy once confessed to a friend that she went to Smith intending to be the most popular and influential girl in her class. Nevertheless, her son recalled many years later that she often mentioned her feeling of awe at the thought of "this little Kansas City girl going to Smith." As class president, she was a member of the Smith College Council. She took an active role in the activities of the Smith Col-

Dorothy at Smith in her senior year

lege Association for Christian Work, and was an officer of the Sociology and Current Events Clubs. Working with the United War Work Campaign, she was instrumental in helping to raise $25,000 for World War I refugees—a most impressive sum in those days. A natural athlete who loved tennis, swimming, hiking, and mountain climbing, Dorothy was also a member of the All-Smith baseball team for three years and played on a class basketball team.

Smith College Class Book, 1919

Dorothy Scarritt, Smith Class of 1919

During her freshman year, Dorothy was fortunate to have a hometown boyfriend at Williams College, fifty miles west of Northampton. Schuyler Ashley, son of a Kansas City lawyer, had attended Country Day, a Kansas City school for boys that was the male equivalent of Barstow. He and Dorothy were part of the same social crowd, attended school and country club dances together, and graduated from high school in the same year. Schuyler stayed at Williams one year, then enlisted in the Navy and served with the North Sea fleet during World War I.

Schuyler contracted tuberculosis and was forced from active duty. He recuperated at a hospital in Leith, Scotland, near the native home of Robert Louis Stevenson, one of his literary heroes and a fellow sufferer from tuberculosis. In 1918 Schuyler returned to the United States and moved to the high dry climate of Colorado Springs to restore his health. He wrote essays, short stories, and book reviews for the *Kansas City Star* and the *Saturday Review of Literature*.

Dorothy graduated from Smith in the spring of 1919, six months after the end of World War I and two months after her 28-year-old sister Frances Margaret died of tuberculosis. Dorothy was devastated by her sister's death and deeply worried about Schuyler's chances for recovery. She corresponded with him regularly and saved every review he later wrote for the *Kansas City Star*.

Despite the darkness and despair in her heart, nothing diminished Dorothy's respect for Smith. She cherished her education and wonderful friends. All her life she loved bright people and was proud to be a "Smith girl." She attended class reunions and kept up with many of her college friends throughout her life.

After graduation, Dorothy went home to her family in Kansas City. She was the Scarritts' youngest child and now their only living daughter. Although she had been encouraged to go east to college, she was expected to come home to marry. Both of her brothers had returned to Kansas City. Bill was married and working in the family real estate and insurance business. A.D. was attending law school there. Dorothy had a wide circle of friends in Kansas City. Her daily schedule, like that of other young women of prominent families, revolved around luncheons, teas, dinner parties, and dances at the country club.

Dorothy, however, was not about to confine her life to Kansas City. In the company of her father and some of her young friends, she traveled widely throughout the world. In July 1921 she made the grand tour of Europe, sailing on the SS *Adriatic*; her travels took her to England, Holland, Switzerland, France, and Italy. The following summer she went to Alaska, the Canadian Rockies, and Yosemite National Park. In July 1924 she visited Newfoundland, Nova Scotia, Quebec, and the Thousand Islands. The following February, she went with her father to Latin America on the SS *Essequibo,* a Pacific mailboat that sailed from New York to Cuba, the Panama Canal, Peru, Chile, and Argentina. Dorothy was an avid photographer and made detailed photo albums of each of her trips.

Chapter 3

THE MCKIBBINS OF ST. PAUL

In September 1923 "Dink," as Dorothy was called by family members and close friends throughout her life, went to White Bear Lake, Minnesota, to visit Alida Bigelow, a Smith College friend. The reunion took place at Dellwood, the summer home of Alida's relatives, the McKibbin family of St. Paul. There Dorothy met Alida's cousin, 30-year-old Joseph Chambers McKibbin, a 1915 graduate of Princeton University who had served in World War I. He had recently left a promising career in investment banking in New York City and returned to St. Paul to learn the family fur business.

The McKibbin family was of Scots-Irish descent, originally from Northern Ireland. They settled first in the Chambersburg area of Pennsylvania. Joseph McKibbin, young Joe's father, was born in Philadelphia and educated in the public schools there. He attended Princeton Academy and Western University in Pittsburgh. In 1877 he went to St. Paul, Minnesota, to live with his older brother Will, then pastor of the Central Presbyterian Church. Eleven years later, after having worked as a bookkeeper for a wholesale mercantile firm and served as field secretary to raise funds for the new Macalester College in St. Paul, Joseph started a fur company, McKibbin & Co. This later became McKibbin,

Driscoll & Dorsey, manufacturers of hats, caps, gloves, plaid woolen mackinaws, and sheepskin-lined coats. The business flourished. Mr. McKibbin was an unsuccessful candidate for mayor of St. Paul on the Republican reform ticket in 1906. He was a trustee of the Central Presbyterian Church and later a member of the House of Hope congregation. He played baseball as a young man and loved the sport all his life.

Joseph married his first wife, Anna Stitt Dorsey, in 1880. She and a baby son died in childbirth four years later, leaving him with a 3-year-old daughter, Allison. In 1887 Joseph married Anna's older sister, Mary Henderson Dorsey. They had five children of their own, two daughters and three sons. Joseph Chambers McKibbin, their middle child, was born in 1893. His brothers, born in 1891 and 1896, each lived a scant year.

Young Joe was a natural athlete and fine sailor. As a child he learned to sail his own boat on White Bear Lake and later crewed for races at the White Bear Yacht Club, earning him the nickname of "Skipper." He prepared for Princeton University at the Hill School in Pottstown, Pennsylvania, where he was captain of the school hockey team.

Joe took an array of courses considered essential for a liberal arts education during his first two years at Princeton. He studied Latin, Greek, and German (languages that he had studied for three years in high school), French, mathematics, physics, psychology, and logic. He majored in economics, complemented by courses in politics, philosophy, history, and English.

Joe, best known as a champion rower, competed on the varsity and class crews throughout his Princeton career. Like Dorothy, he quickly earned recognition as one of the outstanding leaders of his class. His versatile abilities took him into various activities including the Senior Council, the Class Day committee, and Whig Hall, the debating society. President of his alumni class from 1920-25, he was hailed as a "natural ambassador" for Princeton wherever he went. Social life at Princeton in Joe's day revolved around the "eating clubs." Membership in those select organizations determined not only a student's dinner companions in college but also the men with whom he would be associated lifelong. Joe was a member of Ivy, the oldest and most patrician of the eating clubs.

Following graduation Joe returned to St. Paul for one year during which he enlisted in the field artillery. At age 25 and just three years out of college, he was promoted to major and assigned to Fort Sill in Lawton, Oklahoma. Although he was eager to go overseas, the war ended before his unit was called up. Discharged from the Army on December 21, 1918, Joe wrote to his father, "I am a civilian once more with rather a lost ship without a rudder feeling."[1]

After his military service, Joe went to New York City where he joined the investment banking firm of Lee Higginson & Co. He stayed for four years in positions of steadily increasing responsibility, creating the prospect of a successful career in finance. Weekly letters to his family during that period indicate that Joe was enjoying a lively social life with many Princeton classmates and old friends from St. Paul, playing squash regularly, and gaining experience as a bond salesman. In August 1921 he crewed on the White Bear Yacht Club boat that won the race against the Royal St. Lawrence Yacht Club in Montreal. By the spring of 1923, however, he wrote to his parents, "There's been little going on at the office—very dull really and the markets have been going the wrong way to stir up much enthusiasm. The dull periods are bad again— but I guess that's good for us."[2] Shortly after writing that letter, Joe returned to St. Paul to work in the family fur business. By the time Joe and Dorothy met in September 1923, he was well established in the firm and taking on management responsibilities there.

Dorothy and Joe were immediately attracted to each other. Both possessed naturally magnetic personalities. They were strong spirited

Joe McKibbin and Dorothy Scarritt at the time of their engagement

individuals, recognized leaders, and yet both were at crossoads in their lives. Dorothy had been back in Kansas City for four years since her graduation from Smith. She had "seen the world" and longed to be free of the social constraints of her hometown. Although Joe had quickly become an executive partner in his father's business, St. Paul did not offer the free-wheeling life style he had enjoyed in New York.

Dorothy and Joe soon fell in love and became engaged. No records exist to tell us the exact date of that engagement. In the winter of 1925, however, she was diagnosed with tuberculosis. Determined that she would not pass the disease on to any future family members, Dorothy Ann Scarritt broke her engagement to Joseph Chambers McKibbin. That must have been a heartbreaking decision for both of them, and one that Joe would not accept as final.

Chapter 4

SUNMOUNT SANITARIUM

Now the Scarritts were confronted with finding treatment for Dorothy just six years after her sister died in a California sanitarium. They considered many rehabilitation centers before selecting the Sunmount Sanitarium in Santa Fe, New Mexico. At an elevation of 7,000 feet, Santa Fe had a dry, clean atmosphere, reputed to be an essential ingredient in the cure of tuberculosis and other lung ailments. Santa Fe was the state capital and the commercial center for northern New Mexico, one of the most sparsely populated, underdeveloped areas of the United States in 1925.

Sunmount Sanitarium had been established in 1903. It operated as a municipally funded tent city for tuberculosis patients until 1914 when a new facility was built on a small road off Camino del Monte Sol, just north of Old Santa Fe Trail. With the increased availability of rail travel, the number of health seekers, many from the East Coast, grew significantly. Sunmount became a highly respected pulmonary treatment center under the direction of Dr. Frank Mera.

In conventional treatment centers of the 1920s, tuberculosis was considered highly contagious. Patients were isolated from each other

Sunmount Sanitarium in 1925

and the outside world. They were "hospitalized." Dr. Mera, who did not subscribe to that view, promoted Sunmount as a health resort rather than a hospital. Plenty of fresh air and bed rest were the core elements of his treatment. Patients slept outside on screened porches year round. At that time no vaccine or drug regimen existed to kill the microorganism, *M. tuberculosis*, responsible for this deadly disease. Mera had a fatalistic philosophy about the outcome of tuberculosis treatment: many would die; those who lived would be revitalized by their illness. Consequently, he did not quarantine his "guests" but instead filled their days with unique experiences and interesting people.

In November 1925 Dorothy and her mother traveled by train to Santa Fe and took a room at La Fonda. The Scarritts were not aware that there was a waiting list for entrance to Sunmount. It took one month and persuasive advocacy from friends of Dorothy's uncle, Nathan Scarritt, for her to gain admission. She entered Sunmount on December 9.[1]

Dorothy confronted the Sunmount experience with characteristic optimism, hardly acknowledging the dark side of her chronic illness. She had begun writing poetry when she was a student at Barstow, and like many young women of her background in her day, Dorothy often expressed herself in verse:

It's not a melancholy I
who thinks of death.
I crave the gay and reckless world
with wistful breath.
How near we are to dying
Death sees us every day
But life with beauty's crying
I can't go, I must stay.
O life is very merry
and life is very gay
I wonder if I'll lie in bed
Three years from now today?
Gay sun is warmly shining
My sky is blazing blue
The feathered clouds are smiling
Death—get away with you![2]

Her old friend, Schuyler Ashley, with whom she corresponded, marveled at her spirit:

> No one, it seems to me, ever resented the discipline of T.B. less than you did. Your getting it seems a splendid argument, if one is required, for the purposelessness of calamities.
>
> Somehow your letters seem to tell me very little of what I want to know about you (aside from physical news). To talk to you, to watch your face, would be the thing. In your letters I feel an increased appreciation of "still beauty," an even more poignant (God knows it was always sharp enough with you) desire to catch little joys, little happinesses as they go by.[3]

Local Indians were invited to come into Sunmount to dance and sell their dolls, jewelry, small pottery, and rugs. Dorothy bought her first pieces of silver and turquoise jewelry during her sojourn there. Patients went on field trips to northern New Mexico pueblos. Books were passed around, generating lively discussions of world affairs that the well-traveled Dorothy loved.

Instructors from the Santa Fe Art School gave painting classes. On Sunday nights, there was a special program in which writers, poets, musicians, and dancers passing through Santa Fe were invited to read from their works and to entertain.

"Raymond Duncan, the brother of Isadora Duncan, appeared in a sack cloth with a shepherd's crook and told us of his experiences and hopes," Dorothy would recall years later. "People from Russia enlivened us with stories of their theatre and ballet. I fell in love with the place [Sunmount] because of its beauty and the cultural and intellectual atmosphere."[4]

Many artists and writers who came to Sunmount for treatment became permanent Santa Fe residents. They eventually created an arts colony that changed a primitive, sleepy town into a national mecca for creative spirits. Former "lungers" spurred an architectural boom in the 1920s when they bought property and built homes there.

One of the founding members of the colony was Carlos Vierra, a native Californian who had studied painting in San Francisco and New York. Stricken with tuberculosis in 1904, he traveled west seeking a high, dry climate. He recovered at Sunmount and spent the rest of his life in Santa Fe. Vierra, who painted landscapes and historical subjects, was also a skilled photographer. He became a passionate advocate for preserving and restoring old-style adobe buildings.

Vierra was a great influence on John Gaw Meem, another Sunmount patient who had studied civil engineering at the Virginia Military Institute. During his Sunmount stay in the 1920s, Meem spent his days with Vierra studying old photographs and architectural plans. By 1923 Meem had designed his first "Santa Fe Style" home. A few years later, the Santa Fe railroad chose Meem to remodel and enlarge La Fonda. In 1933 he was appointed architect for the University of New Mexico and subsequently designed more than thirty buildings on that campus. Meem became the premier architect of Santa Fe and the central influence in the restoration and preservation of early colonial structures. He built his own house on a piece of land he had admired from his bed on the Sunmount porch.

Alice Corbin, a Chicago poet and an associate editor of *Poetry: A Magazine of Modern Verse*, moved to New Mexico in 1916 with her husband, William Penhallow Henderson. A Sunmount patient on several occasions, she invited Carl Sandburg and Vachel Lindsay to read from their work, and she read her own poetry to appreciative audiences. The Hendersons settled in Santa Fe and became leaders of the arts colony. William, an artist best known for his paintings of New Mexican landscapes, also designed furniture and worked as an architect.

In 1922 Witter Bynner, a Harvard graduate, poet, and prolific author, came to Sunmount to visit Alice Corbin and recover from influenza. When he arrived, after a ten-month stay in China, he was working on *The Jade Mountain*, a translation of an anthology of T'ang dynasty poems that was published in 1929 and widely acknowledged as a major contribution to 20th century literature. Bynner bought a house in Santa Fe where he lived until his death in 1968. He was a personable host who opened his house regularly to artistic people in all fields. D.H. and Frieda Lawrence were among his first house guests. A patron of the arts and strong supporter of Indian rights, he was at the center of the literary and political ferment of the 1920s and 1930s.

Two other Sunmount alumni, Gerald Cassidy and Sheldon Parsons, were important Southwest painters who stayed in Santa Fe after their health improved. Cassidy, a commercial artist from New York, painted western scenes that were reproduced on postcards and Santa Fe railway travel posters. He was also a serious painter of northern New Mexico vistas. His paintings of landscapes and Indians were purchased by many museums across the country, including the New York Museum of Art. Like Cassidy, Parsons, formerly a portrait painter from New York, concentrated on landscapes but rendered them in an impressionistic style. He became director of the state art museum in Santa Fe in 1918.

Dorothy, with her cheerful, outgoing personality, made many friends in the Santa Fe arts colony during her Sunmount stay. She also acquired a passion and appreciation for the native arts of northern New Mexico. Little did the Scarritts know when they chose Sunmount for Dorothy's treatment that they were providing her with both the most effective medical care available and a cultural experience that would come to dominate her life.

Dorothy's Sunmount stay was blessedly short. She achieved the status of "cured" in one scant year. Toward the end of that year, Dr. Mera gave Joe McKibbin permission to visit Dorothy. Although no letters of this period survive, it is evident that the two had remained in close contact. While Joe was in New Mexico, they renewed their plans to marry. Dorothy left the sanitarium on December 22, 1926, and returned home to Kansas City to prepare for her wedding. The Sunmount experience had saved her life and markedly changed the course of it.

Early in January 1927, Dorothy received a letter from Schuyler Ashley:

> Dearest Dor:—
>
> Luck for the New Year, my dear! We are fighting on to some line though, it seems, fatal not to see or help each other enough. At least I'm not able to, and it's a sorrow to me. I remember you in days of my deepest depression, four years ago…
>
> I took cold two days after Xmas, began to nose dive, and thought I was going to be really gravely sick, but here I am bobbing up wanly and serenely again…
>
> For God's sake take care of yourself, my dear. Remember you are fragile and unique every second.
>
> Love, SA[5]

One month later, Dorothy's great joy in her recovery and engagement to Joe McKibbin was diminished by Schuyler's sudden, unexpected death. He died of a heart attack on January 25, 1927.

Chapter 5

MARRIAGE AND MOVING ON

In the late afternoon of Wednesday, October 5, 1927, Dorothy Ann Scarritt and Joseph Chambers McKibbin were married in the garden of her family home in Kansas City. Given the social prominence of the Scarritts, this wedding might have been the social event of the year, conducted at the Melrose Methodist Episcopal Church with a country club reception. However, Dorothy, nearly 30 years old, and Joe, 34, had a small, very personal celebration, followed by a wedding supper attended by immediate family members and close friends.

The local society weekly noted that "expressing distinct individuality in her wedding gown, Dorothy Ann Scarritt chose a sapphire blue velvet dress and wore a small hat to match. She carried a shower bouquet of orchids, blue delphinium, and lilies of the valley."[1] On their honeymoon, Dorothy and Joe went by ship from New York to Rio de Janeiro. In Rio they were guests of Dorothy's matron of honor, Jean van Gelder, a Smith friend, and her husband, Hendrik Pieter. The newlyweds returned from their wedding trip in early December.

They spent the winter, the snowiest on record since 1880, at Dellwood, the McKibbin family home at White Bear Lake, Minnesota,

Joe and Dorothy with their dog, Peter the Great, at the time of their marriage

Dorothy in her blue wedding dress

The winter after their marriage, Joe and Dorothy purchased this house on Princeton Avenue in St. Paul.

where they had met in 1923. Joe continued to work with his father in the family fur business. By the next winter, the young McKibbins had purchased a house on Princeton Avenue, a street of handsome homes in a well-established St. Paul neighborhood.

On December 6, 1930, they were blessed with a son, Kevin. Eight days after his birth, Dorothy wrote this piece for her new son:

> None of this 'valley of the shadow of death' but peaks of excitement of life.
>
> Born from the earthquake, the wind and the sea and the mountains and singing torn skies. Color and sound and motion.
>
> I was just a hotel where he stopped for a while.
>
> He belongs to no tribe, no race, no people. He belongs to himself, which is a familiar of high singing places.
>
> He must not be tarnished and worn by people. He must stay in the sunlight. His feet shall be ever moving, moving about the earth which is his.
>
> There is nothing personal about happiness. It is an aliveness. It is a oneness with nature and with humanity. It is a deep knowledge of suffering and desolation. It is an intenseness of feeling, of understanding of good and evil. Compassion. Vital awareness of being a part of the universe in all its manifestations. Harmony. Acute knowledge of kinship with all the peoples of the earth. Recognition of true values. Preoccupation with truth.[2]

In May Joe and Dorothy drove with Kevin to Kansas City. Dorothy had nursed Kevin for five months and now was leaving him for the first time with her parents. She and Joe motored on to the mountains of Colorado and revisited Santa Fe. Joe "was taken with the New Mexico country and decided that someday they would settle there, where they could have horses and dogs and raise their family under the incredible blue skies and golden sun."[3] Another goal was that one day they would move to New York City, and Joe would return to his work in the financial world as an investment banker.

Both of those dreams were shattered on October 27, 1931, when Joseph Chambers McKibbin died of Hodgkin's disease, an uncommon cancer of the lymphatic system. His memorial service was held at home in St. Paul.

In the *Princeton Alumni Weekly,* November 3, 1931, the secretary for his class remembered Joe McKibbin. "Joe's life was characterized in an exceptional degree by those qualities of sincerity, loyalty, courage, and sportsmanship which commanded the respect and high esteem of a host of friends recruited from all walks of life, and which endeared him to every member of his class."[4]

Writing about Joe in 1965, in celebration of what would have been his fiftieth reunion at Princeton, another classmate noted, "No biography of Joe would be complete without mentioning 'Dink,' his devoted and courageous wife, who nursed him during the long and hopeless illness of Hodgkin's disease."[5]

Dorothy mentioned in a personal unpublished manuscript (writing about herself and Joe in the third person) that "they had been married only half over a year when he was struck with Hodgkin's disease. He was never told of his terminal illness."[6] Joe may have never been "told," but it is hard to believe that a man as smart and sensitive as Joe McKibbin did not know the nature of his illness. More likely, his magnetic charm and Dorothy's positive spirit helped him triumph over despair while he kept his fears to himself. The summer trip west in 1931 occurred in the waning days of Joe's life, yet Dorothy and Joe wove dreams about their future.

Dorothy kept a journal of Kevin's first five years that she named "The Book of Kevin McKibbin." "His father was in bed four months," she wrote, "and the little boy played around on his bed, climbed over him, and pulled at his buttons on the green and lavender pajamas. He would crawl across the floor to the bed. And laugh all the time. His tub was arranged so that his father could see him in it from his bed. Such splashings!"[7]

There was no laughter in Dorothy during Joe's final days. In anguish she wrote this undated poem:

Dorothy and Joe admire their new baby.

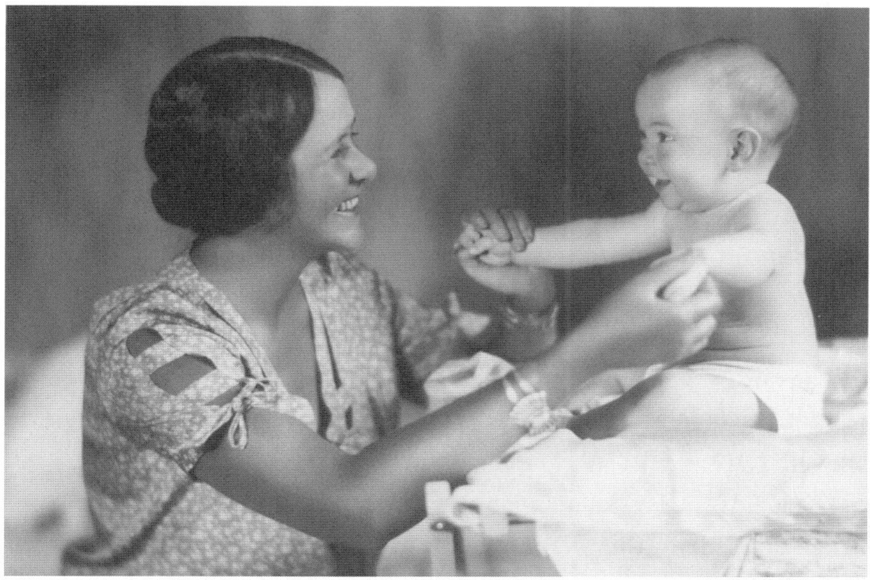

Dorothy and Kevin at play, enjoying the delight in each other that sustained them lifelong

He is not dead, he's dying
For months he's been that way
He will not let me see him.
He did not smile today.

I am an outcast driven
Into the world alone.
Why can't I stumble weary
Into his arms my home.
Joan of Arc bound down her head
To sob
She was discouraged.
And then she raised her head again
And went on with a flourish.

I am no Joan, and yet
I knew
Her treacherous entourage.
No matter what our grade or rank
We must go on with courage.[8]

Dorothy made the decision to leave St. Paul shortly after Joe's death. The Princeton Avenue house, because of its location and desirability, probably sold quickly. In all of Dorothy's writings, there is no reference to the sale of the house or the income from it. She does mention having only a small insurance pension to support herself and young son. Princeton classmates and other friends set up a trust fund for Kevin's college education.

Some six weeks after Joe's funeral, Dorothy took Kevin and Peter the Great, their greyhound, to Kansas City. On Christmas Day, Kevin took his first step alone. The Scarritts expected Dorothy and Kevin to stay in Kansas City permanently and live with them at their 3240 Norledge Avenue residence. Offering her the ballroom on the third floor for an apartment, they wanted her to return to her roots, to an ordered life in a milieu where she was known and loved, and to a family who would help her raise Kevin in the Scarritt tradition. Given her strong family ties, her revered place in their world, and the loneliness and despair she must have felt, it would have been a logical move for her.

Dorothy had been away from Kansas City for only four years when Joe died. She was a loving daughter who respected her parents and wanted to please them, but she knew that she did not want to settle permanently in Kansas City. She did not want to compromise her hard-earned freedom, gained from her experiences at Smith College, at Sunmount Sanitarium, and in St. Paul. She did not want to live under her parents' roof and return to a way of life she found confining. She did not want to wear a hat and gloves all her life.

Dorothy stayed at home until mid-March, then returned to St. Paul. Over the next six weeks, she put her affairs in order. Guided by the dream that she and Joe shared of raising a family in northern New Mexico, Dorothy loaded her baby and their worldly belongings into a Model A coupe and drove to Santa Fe. Joe's sister, Maggie McKibbin, traveled with them on a trip that took nearly a month. They arrived on June 11, 1932.

Part Two
RETURN TO SANTA FE

Chapter 6

CREATING A NEW LIFE

Dorothy's return to Santa Fe brought her back to the climate and vistas she loved and to Sunmount friends who welcomed her and gave her entrée to a fascinating new world in the arts. Although he was too little to understand, she told Kevin that they were going to a place where they would "sit under a piñon tree and spend all their days in peace and happiness." Later she wrote, "Little did I realize that 'under a piñon tree'...would become one of the most sensitive areas of the world."[1]

At this time, only some 12,000 people lived in Santa Fe and life moved at a leisurely pace. The cost of living in New Mexico was among the lowest in the country. In 1925 a two- or three-room adobe house in Santa Fe rented for less than $10 a month.[2] Dorothy noted that "from a practical viewpoint, her bit of money would go further there, at least take care of them until Kevin was old enough for nursery school and she could take employment."[3]

Dorothy chose to live in El Zaguan, an old hacienda off the unpaved Canyon Road, an ancient Indian trail along the Santa Fe River. Woodcutters, accompanied by burros with the spicy smelling piñon

El Zaguan on Canyon Road

stacked on their backs, used the trail to bring firewood down from the mountains. The wood cost 50 cents a stack; the burro, $5. El Zaguan, one of the architectural treasures of New Mexico, took its name from the long covered corridor that ran from the large garden at the west to an open patio on the east.[4] At one time the house contained twenty-four rooms, with servants' quarters across the street. By the time Dorothy arrived, it had been converted into rental apartments. Dorothy was charmed by her modest sunny new home with a small living room, one bedroom, bath, and kitchen with a gas stove and refrigerator. It was set in a walled courtyard, surrounded by lilacs, phlox, and tamarisk. There was a fountain in the center where Kevin and Peter the Great played and "swam." They stayed there through the winter and in 1933 moved into a larger two-bedroom, adobe-style guest house on the same property.

One of Dorothy's first friends was Peggy Pond Church, the wife of Fermor Church, a master at Los Alamos Ranch School founded by Peggy's father, Ashley Pond Jr. The school, thirty-five miles northwest of Santa Fe, was isolated on the Pajarito (Little Bird) Plateau in the

T. Harmon Parkhurst photo,Courtesy Museum of New Mexico Neg. 14148

Woodcutters with their piñon-loaded burros on Shelby Street

Jemez Mountains. Peggy, as a faculty wife, had Indian or Hispanic women from the nearby valley who lived in, helped cook, and took care of her three sons, leaving her time to write poetry and explore on horseback the mountains she loved. When she and Dorothy met, she was beginning an association with the Santa Fe Writers' Colony and was to become a distinguished writer and "first lady of New Mexico poetry."[5] Dorothy and Peggy shared a common bond in their affiliation with Smith College. Peggy, six years younger than Dorothy, attended Smith from 1922 until her marriage in 1924. Although they were not on the campus at the same time, they studied there in a similar period and perhaps took some of the same courses with the same professors.

Dorothy and Kevin spent two weeks at the Ranch School with Peggy and her family in July 1932. Peggy took them to Otowi—which in the Indians' Tewa language means "the place where the water makes a noise"—to meet Edith Warner, another remarkable woman who had come west to restore her health and live a quiet life.[6] For more than twenty years Edith lived in a small adobe house on San Ildefonso Pueblo land beside the Rio Grande with the nearby Indians as her only neighbors. She had a tea room there, and Atilano Montoya, "Tilano," former governor and distinguished elder of the pueblo, came to live with her.

Although they were temperamentally direct opposites, Dorothy and Edith became good friends. Edith, shy and prim, craved simplicity in her life. Dorothy loved being at the center of things. She greatly admired Edith. "Her personality was so appealing that many poets and writers consulted her about their work and hopes," Dorothy wrote. "She filled one with her spirit of kindness and strength and peace and humor. She inspired everyone who talked with her."[7]

Many friends and family members visited Dorothy and Kevin that first year at El Zaguan. Over the summer, her father came out twice from Kansas City, and Mother McKibbin, Kevin's St. Paul grandmother, visited in October. Dorothy set up an annual routine of leaving Santa Fe by train in mid-December, visiting the Scarritts for Christmas, then traveling on to the McKibbins. This tradition, with minor variations, lasted throughout Kevin's childhood. Dorothy loved those visits to St. Paul, which she described as that "peaceful sweet sad place."[8] She wrote about them in detail, giving a sense of the warmth and joy she found in the McKibbins' love for her and their grandson. Father McKibbin adored Kevin and sent him charming letters and drawings.

In the winter of 1933, they returned to Kansas City after the St. Paul stay. Three days after their arrival, Kevin, now 27 months old, came down with scarlet fever. "Poor little baby," Dorothy wrote, "burning up with fever, rash all over, bad cough like whooping cough...throat too sore to swallow."[9] Dorothy and a staff of nurses cared for him at the Scarritts until Dorothy became ill with a flu virus and needed nursing care herself. It was the middle of March before they could travel. Kevin was train-sick and fretful en route to Santa Fe. But the sun was shining when they arrived, welcoming them home, and reaffirming Dorothy's decision to create a new life in a land of brilliant blue skies away from the darkness of St. Paul and the constraints of Kansas City.

T. Harmon Parkhurst, Courtesy Museum of New Mexico Neg 118249

A fiesta parade passes by the Spanish and Indian Trading Company on East San Francisco Street.

On May 1 Kevin started "school" in a morning play group of six children. Dorothy took a part-time job as bookkeeper for the Spanish and Indian Trading Company, located across the street from La Fonda, where she and her mother had stayed awaiting her entrance to Sunmount. Vivian Martinez, whom Kevin called "Nana," helped Dorothy with household chores and cared for Kevin in her absence.

The Spanish and Indian Trading Company was owned by Norman McGee and Jim McMillan. They paid Dorothy 50 cents an hour to keep the accounts and pay the bills. "While they were tossing out $10,000 here and $10,000 there for consignments of art treasures," she said, "they were prone to forget to pay the rent. As for balanced books, they were too much in demand on the social scene to attend to such mundane matters. That was left to me."[10] The position was a perfect fit for Dorothy and heightened her passion for Indian arts and crafts.

"It was the most noted [store] of its kind in New Mexico, perhaps in the entire Southwest," she wrote. "Indians from all the pueblos, from the Navajo reservations and the Hopi villages brought their finest blankets, their pottery and woven baskets of museum caliber, to trade. Spanish traders brought hand-carved furniture and the rarest of old santos, bultos, and retablos [wooden religious portraits, sculptures and paintings]."[11]

Although Dorothy had an interesting job and a growing circle of friends, Kevin was always the center of her universe.

On New Year's Day 1934, Dorothy took Kevin to the San Ildefonso Pueblo to see his first Indian dance, and she was curious to see his reaction. When he first saw and heard the Indians singing, he approached them silently. Mother and son sat on the bare earth, feet out in front, and watched them dance. Kevin was reverent and still, unlike his usual exuberant 3-year-old self. When it was over and they were walking to the car, Kevin said, "Indians go boomp [the drum]," and then he danced. "What will the Indians do now, Diedee?" "The Indians will have their supper; the Indians will go to sleep." "Don't suck your thumb, Indians!" little Kevin admonished.[12]

At the end of May they moved into a house on Barcelona Road. There were stunning mountain views in three directions. "We see the Sangre de Cristos in the purple light," Dorothy noted. "And the Jemez, lavender and glowing under the sun. And the Sandias, misty and beckoning, over their floating gold." "Oh, see the lights of the town," Kevin said.[13]

In June Dorothy and Kevin went to St. Paul. Dorothy left Kevin with the McKibbins while she attended her fifteenth reunion at Smith and traveled in the east visiting old friends. She was gone for nearly one month. Kevin had a wonderful time with the McKibbin clan. He stayed at his Aunt Allison's house under the care of Lola Gresham who became his great friend. He went swimming in White Bear Lake. He and his grandfather took long walks together and rode on the streetcar. He picked flowers for his grandmother. Late in the month, Miss Gresham took him by train to Kansas City where he was reunited with his mother. Just before her arrival, a heavy door on the Scarritt's Cadillac closed on his thumb, cracking the thumb bone in three places. It was put in a splint. Pauline, the family maid, re-bandaged the thumb and replaced the splint. After she was all through, Kevie held it up very carefully and said, "Joke! You put it on the wrong thumb!"[14]

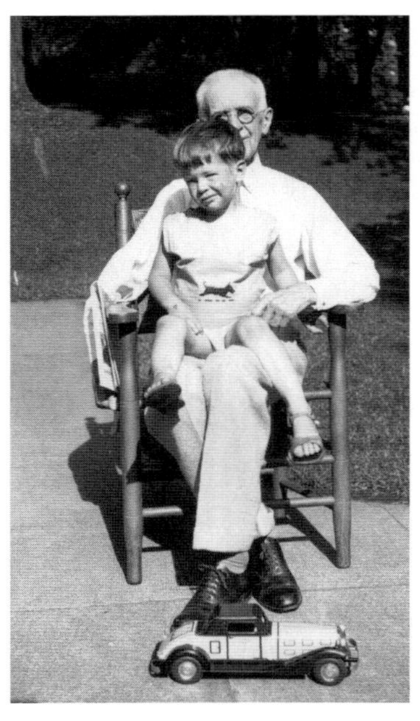

Kevin with his grandfather in St. Paul

In the fall of 1934, the number of children in the nursery school group increased to ten, and there were structured activities, more like a kindergarten. Kevin went in the morning, five days a week. Lillian, a black woman, worked for them as a mother's helper. Kevin thought Lillian was very sunburned. He sat out in the sun, hoping his skin would be like hers. He found a freckle on his back and said, "Am I getting brown like Lillian?"[15]

In those days—and throughout Kevin's growing-up years—there were many family pets, often on a rotating basis. A black and white kitten, given to him by Edith Warner, quickly disappeared. Dorothy went back to Edith's house and came home with two gray and white kittens. His Kansas City grandmother sent him a little green turtle that got lost after only ten days. One Easter he had three rabbits he and Dorothy selected from a nearby store that gave away one rabbit with each $5 purchase. Dogs got into the rabbit pen, and two escaped. The third, Cottontail, remained but lost a good bit of hair. Kevin tried to glue more cotton on its tail. Happily, the storekeeper replaced the lost bunnies. Two short-lived chicks were also a part of the Easter menagerie. The one constant was Peter the Great, then 10 years old, who went everywhere with them, including Kansas City and St. Paul.

On weekends Dorothy drove Kevin all over northern New Mexico. She photographed old houses and sketched traditional architectural features. When she saw something being torn down, she bought the windows, gates, doors, vigas, and corbels, often rescuing them from dump heaps. She bought collections of pieces that came into the Spanish and Indian Trading Company. She got wooden tables, old chairs, and tinwork from a shop around the corner between La Fonda and the cathedral. Her photography, sketching, and collecting were all part of a dream to build a house in Santa Fe one day.

Dorothy, Kevin, and Peter the Great

Kevin with one of his favorite pets

The spring of 1935 brought change to Dorothy and Kevin's comfortable routine. Kevin's small nursery school closed, and Lillian left their employment. In May Dorothy gave up her job at the Spanish and Indian Trading Company. She stayed at home with

Kevin for more than a year until August 31, 1936, when he officially started school. They had a wonderful time, spending four weeks in Kansas City at Christmas, followed by two weeks in St. Paul.

Upon their return, Dorothy commissioned Katherine Stinson Otero to draw up the plans for a house. Katherine Stinson was one of the most skilled and respected pioneer aviators in the United States. She is credited with being the first woman to skywrite, fly air mail, and fly solo at night. Born in 1891, she started flying as a teenager in Texas and was the fourth woman in history to receive a pilot's license, issued in 1912. Suffering from tuberculosis, Katherine came to Sunmount in the early 1920s when John Gaw Meem was a patient there. Based on their fascination with the cultural and artistic heritage of New Mexico, they developed a close and enduring friendship. As her health improved, Katherine began remodeling old buildings and designing new ones in the Pueblo Revival Style championed by Meem. The key design elements of that style came from the architecture of the pueblos, mission churches, Spanish colonial buildings and fortifications. Like Meem, she was not trained professionally as an architect, yet her work quickly gained wide recognition and garnered awards in state-wide design competitions. In 1927 she married Miguel Otero Jr., son of one of New Mexico's territorial governors and a lawyer who served in a number of state political offices.

Mr. Scarritt came often to check on construction.

On April 21, 1936, Dorothy purchased one and a half acres of land in the sandy piñon-covered hills south of the old city of Santa Fe, near Sunmount Sanitarium.[16] The cost of land and building the house was $10,000. Given Dorothy's modest salary and small insurance pension, her father may have helped with the financing. He came out to Santa Fe on several occasions to observe the progress of the house construction.

Katherine Otero and Dorothy collaborated on the plan for the McKibbin house. Although the Pueblo Revival Style was fashionable in Santa Fe, Dorothy wanted her house to be an authentic copy of a typical New Mexico Hispanic farm or ranch house of the late 19th and early 20th centuries. The house Katherine Otero designed for her carefully replicated such a traditional structure and looked "as if it had been built by accretion over several hundred years."[17] The thick-walled adobe house, which is now on the National Register of Historic Places, is U-shaped in plan with a flat, parapeted roof. The front portal, supported by carved corbels, is 65 feet long and 10 feet wide, stretching almost the entire length of the house.

The building of his new house was an extraordinary experience for a 5-year-old boy. "We were out there every day," Kevin recalls. " I loved seeing what was going on, all the work that was being put into it. I especially loved watching the whole crew of Indian workers peeling aspens for the living room ceiling."[18]

The new house under construction

The new house promised spectacular views.

Laura Gilpin,1948

The completed portal stretches almost the length of the house.

Dorothy and Kevin moved into their house on what is now Old Santa Fe Trail in the fall of 1936, soon after Kevin started school. He was allowed to enter the first grade although he did not celebrate his sixth birthday until December. He attended the Gormley School, which was located about halfway between their new home and the Spanish and Indian Trading Company where Dorothy had returned to work. She drove Kevin to school, picked him up and brought him home for lunch, and returned for him when the school day ended. Sometimes she took him home and left him alone until her work was completed for the day; other times she took him down to the Spanish and Indian Trading Company for the afternoon. Kevin vividly remembers her office there. "Off to one side, there was a little side room where my mother held forth, and she had a desk that reminded me of Scrooge's desk. It was a high desk and she sat on a high stool with a huge ledger in front of her. She had a bare light bulb there that just hung down from a string."[19]

In the summer between first and second grade, the family doctor diagnosed Kevin with rheumatic endocarditis, a potentially fatal heart disease. Kevin remained home in bed for the entire 1937-38 school year. He was not allowed any physical activity. Kevin stayed in bed, listening to the radio, reading, playing with small toys, and enjoying his own company. Dorothy came home for lunch and went back to work in the afternoon. Each day various friends stopped by and checked on Kevin. During this whole period of time, he never felt sick. It was a sad and stressful year for Dorothy: her son bed-ridden with a life-threatening illness, the loss of her father who died of bronchial pneumonia on February 16, 1938, and the death of Mother McKibbin five days later.

In the summer of 1938, to Kevin's delight and relief, Dorothy decided to take him to the Los Angeles Children's Hospital for a reassessment of his illness. Kevin's grandmother and his aunt, Nana, came from Kansas City to "chaperone" Dorothy and Kevin on this journey.

Mrs. Scarritt and her sister arrived in a LaSalle, driven by a liveried chauffeur. Dorothy and Kevin drove in their car, followed by the LaSalle. The Kansas City contingent stayed until Dorothy found suitable lodging, a little house in Long Beach, one block from the beach. Kevin has clear memories of that journey:

> We stopped at San Bernardino, the second or third day on the road. It was about mid-morning, and I got out of the car to run around. There were a lot of little Spanish American kids there. I stopped and started playing with them and talking to them, because it was just like home for me.
>
> My great aunt, Nana, called to me. She was very debilitated with arthritis and almost a complete invalid. Nana told me to come over to her. She stomped her cane and told me to 'stop associating with those blue-blacks.' And I will never forget that!
>
> I remember when we were first approaching the ocean. I was so excited. I was beside myself. I didn't see it until we came around a bend on this road. We were on the bluff, and there it was, down there! There was a long series of steps going down to the water—-and I wasn't supposed to do it—but I just took off and ran down the steps and out to the ocean. Then I came running back up this thing, which according to all the doctors should have killed me, but it didn't.[20]

Dorothy and Kevin spent a wonderful summer in Long Beach. Kevin went to the Los Angeles Children's Hospital for evaluation. The doctors there discovered that he had a severe case of tonsillitis. They removed his tonsils, and he was "cured"!

It is a puzzle how Dorothy managed that summer without an income and with rent and doctors' bills to pay. Knowing the McKibbins' adoration for Kevin and Dorothy, it seems likely that they helped financially in time of need. We can also hypothesize that Dorothy had an inheritance from Mr. Scarritt. He may have sequestered some funds for Dorothy and his grandson. However, when his will was probated in May 1939, there was not sufficient money to cover his considerable debts, let alone enough to provide for his wife. After his assets were liquidated and the Norledge Avenue house sold, Mrs. Scarritt was forced to move into a small apartment with her older sister, Nana. It was an abrupt change from their chauffeured cross-country trip the previous summer.

Family members note that although Mr. Scarritt had a successful corporate law practice, he was "in and out" of money. His money problems may have been compounded by an addition to the Melrose Methodist Church built on land donated by Nathan Scarritt. In 1928 eleven Kansas City men made a commitment to raise $140,000 for a new chapel. It was agreed among them that if any one of the eleven could not pay his share, the rest would "ante up." It is likely that Scarritt, as one of the shareholders, was forced to assume the debts of others.

In the fall of 1938, Kevin entered the second grade, and Dorothy returned to her work at the Spanish and Indian Trading Company. Kevin loved living on the outer edge of Santa Fe. He made his own entertainment. He liked to "potter around," [Kevin's words] wandering in the brush, looking for snakes, horny toads, and lizards. He loved to play with small cars and trucks and, as an adult, remains "crazy about automobiles."

Courtesy Museum of New Mexico, Neg. No. 148145

Katherine Stinson and Mike Otero

Katherine and Mike Otero became great friends of the McKibbins. The Oteros had no children of their own and were very kind to Kevin. It was a special treat for him to go to their spacious home in downtown Santa Fe. In August 1939, they invited Dorothy and Kevin to go with them out into the Hopi country to see the annual snake dance. The trip was a memorable one. In a large, old Packard sedan, pulling a little trailer behind, they covered miles of unpaved roads. They arrived in the evening and camped out overnight. The next day they watched the dance, an impressive, all-afternoon event, calling on the spirits to send rain. By the time the dance was over, the rains had come! The foursome took off immediately, but given the downpour and the condition of the roads, they moved very slowly. Fortunately, the roads were sandy, not muddy. At one o'clock in the morning, they pulled into a large Indian hospital at Ganado, Arizona. The attendants there let them sleep on the floor of a hospital room. This adventure was the start of an annual tradition that lasted over the next decade, uninterrupted by gas rationing or World War II.

The Oteros, Peggy Pond Church, and Edith Warner were part of Dorothy's circle of close friends. Former Sunmount "guests" Witter Bynner and John Gaw Meem introduced her to leaders of the Santa Fe arts colony. She and Kevin were frequent guests at Witter's home. His partner, Bobby, was a great storyteller whose tales delighted Kevin.

John Gaw Meem and his wife, Faith, lived within walking dis-

T. Harmon Parkhurst, Courtesy Museum of New Mexico Neg. No. 10692

La Fonda, the hotel at the end of the Santa Fe Trail, in the 1930s

tance of the McKibbins. Faith, a Bostonian and trained architect, shared her husband's passion for historic preservation and was dedicated to retaining the early character of Santa Fe. She was also a founder of the Santa Fe Maternal and Child Health Center, created to dispense birth control devices and information. The center was supported by many in the arts community, including Dorothy.

In 1926, John Gaw Meem and other civic-minded residents formed the Old Santa Fe Association. The center of its mission was "to preserve and maintain the ancient landmarks, historical structures and traditions of Old Santa Fe [and] to guide its growth and development."[21] By joining that group shortly after her return in 1932, Dorothy put herself at the center of the preservation cause.

Another of Dorothy's friends was Emily Otis. In 1927 Emily's brother, Raymond Otis, a novelist, had come from Chicago to settle in the writers' colony. His work drew on local subjects and included *Fire in the Night*, one of the first books to deal with the cultural mix of Santa Fe society. Emily visited him often over the next decade. They were

T. Harmon Parkhurst photo Courtesy Museum of New Mexico Neg. No.54316

La Fonda lobby was a popular gathering place in the 1930s.

great friends of Dorothy's bosses at the Spanish and Indian Trading Company. Emily loved to "hang out" at the store and met Dorothy there. Emily noted that Dorothy, like Raymond, quickly became a part of the literary and artistic scene, which was small in those days and concentrated on the east side of Santa Fe. "I don't remember anything overwhelming when I met Dorothy," Emily recalled. "She silently just came into our lives, and my brother and I loved Dorothy. She was a sweet and beautiful person. She was kind with an unconditional approach when she met people."[22]

In 1931 Emily Otis married Nathaniel Owings, one of the founding partners of the Chicago architectural firm, Skidmore, Owings and Merrill. She was in and out of Santa Fe and saw a great deal of Dorothy until Raymond's death in 1938. The two women were then separated until the Owings moved to a small, thirty-acre ranch in Pojoaque, northwest of Santa Fe, eight years later. Their neighbor was Cady Wells, another devoted friend of Dorothy and Kevin, who remembers him as a "great, great guy."

Cady Wells was one of the Southwest's most distinguished artists. Best known as a water colorist, his paintings are in the permanent collections of a number of national museums, including the Boston Museum of Fine Arts and the Fogg Museum at Harvard. He was a member of the Wells family of Sturbridge, Massachusetts, founders of the American Optical Company, the largest U.S. manufacturer of optical goods, and Old Sturbridge Village, a living museum portraying early village life in New England. He attended eastern preparatory schools and Harvard before he broke from the family expectations and went to New Mexico to paint in 1927. The Owings, Dorothy, and Cady saw each other regularly. "Cady was our best friend, and Dorothy was our best friend, so it became sort of a foursome," Emily recalled. "She was so wise.... They were very, very close; they nearly married."[23]

Dorothy met Martha Graham, the legendary dancer, choreographer and teacher, who spent her summers in Pojoaque in the late 1930s. Martha toured the United States for four years, 1932-1935, in a dance production of *Electra.* During that time she became fascinated with the Indians of the Southwest and the history of the American west, motifs that she incorporated into her dance repertoire. The two women kept in touch over four decades. In 1979, when Dorothy celebrated her sixtieth reunion at Smith, she drove from Northampton to New York City, where, at Martha's invitation, she attended a dress rehearsal of two ballets Martha was preparing for an international tour of Europe, Egypt, and the Middle East.

Laura Gilpin, the photographer who chronicled the landscape of the Southwest and southwestern Indian life, took many childhood pictures of Kevin and did classic photos of the McKibbin Santa Fe house. Born in Colorado Springs in 1891, Laura studied photography in New York for two years until a bad case of influenza sent her home to recover. For more than sixty-five years, she roamed the most remote areas of the Southwest with her camera. She was a trusted friend of the Navajo, who allowed her to go places and photograph things that few Anglos ever saw. These images are recorded in *The Enduring Navajo*, her most famous collection.

Dorothy, with the confidence to trust her intuitions, had a strong social radar that brought her into the company of fascinating people throughout her life. Frances Hawkins, one of Dorothy's dearest friends, spoke with clear insight when she said, "Dorothy had an uncanny, glorious ability to find the good people whom she could look up to, and others she could live with. But she was never fooled by anybody."[24]

Chapter 7

CHANGING JOBS

On May 10, 1940, Dorothy was in the Indian village of Supai on the floor of the Grand Canyon when she heard the news of Germany's invasion of Holland. Cady Wells, Eliot Porter, and his wife, Aline, were with her. Eliot Porter, a master nature photographer, pioneered the use of color in outdoor photography. He would achieve national prominence in 1962 with the publication of *In Wildness Is the Preservation of the World,* a collection of seasonal photographs of northeastern woods, ponds, marshes, and streams and selected passages from the writings of Henry David Thoreau. Dorothy would later describe the occasion:

> The four of us, sitting in front of a mound of fried eggs, heard the 8:00 a.m. announcement [on the radio] that the Germans had marched into Holland. There was a moment of stunned disbelief.
>
> How strange it was, the sky was just as blue, the wild celery stood in the streams as before, [the water] rushed into Havasu Falls, and crystal shimmered on the backs of frogs leaping in and out of the stream.
>
> Everything was the same. But nothing would be the same again. There would never again be a piñon tree under which there was eternal peace and everlasting happiness.[1]

Just over eighteen months later when the United States entered World War II, Dorothy decided she wanted to have some part in the defense effort. However, she was uncertain how to become involved in a significant way. Her responsibilities as mother and provider meant that she could not be separated from Kevin, and her roots were now in Santa Fe. In 1943 when her employers closed the Spanish and Indian Trading Company to enter war-related work, she was out of a job. Perplexed about what to do next, she applied first at the bank where she knew the president, George Bloom, a good friend from Sunmount days. He promptly said that at 45 she was too old. A week or so later he called to say that there was an opening in his loan department, and that if she took a Civil Service exam and got on the Register, he could consider her. Her response: "But I'm too old!"[2]

Although George Bloom did not exactly come out and say it, he had realized that most of the men were going off to war and that young male help would become scarce. Dorothy took the typing exam in the basement of the post office and failed it. She noted, "I was trying to type so fast that I ran off the lines, and the old machine did nothing to help. No bells rang; no horns blew."[3] Not accustomed to failure, Dorothy was so infuriated that five days later she took the test again and passed it. She was immediately offered the position at the bank. Maintaining her pride, she told Bloom she would think it over.

It was in that period of "thinking it over," late March 1943, that Dorothy was introduced to Robert Oppenheimer in the lobby of La Fonda. With no further thought of the secure bank position, she instantly decided to risk her future on an unknown enterprise. Why? Who was this J. Robert Oppenheimer, whose magnetism and charm so intrigued the sensible, responsible Dorothy McKibbin that she seized the opportunity to work with him, whoever he was, whatever he did?

Chapter 8

J. ROBERT OPPENHEIMER

J. Robert Oppenheimer was born in New York City on April 22, 1904, the first son of Julius and Ella Friedman Oppenheimer. What the "J" in Robert's name stood for has long been a subject of conjecture. One version is that "Julius first intended calling him simply Robert, but feeling that this was lacking in distinction, added his own initial at the front—J. Robert Oppenheimer."[1] In his obituary in the *New York Times*, Oppenheimer is referred to as "J (for nothing) Robert Oppenheimer."[2] From the moment she met him, Dorothy called him "Robert."

Julius Oppenheimer came from Germany in 1888, at age 17, to work in a textile importing business owned by relatives who, like himself, were of European-Jewish descent. To meet the demand of a newly developing ready-to-wear clothing industry, he formed his own company that specialized in importing men's suit linings. By the time he was 30, he was a relatively prosperous man. As his command of English grew, he read widely and developed an interest in the arts. In 1903 Oppenheimer married Ella Friedman. A painter of some distinction, Ella had studied in Paris and was teaching in her own studio in New York at the time of her marriage.

Los Alamos Historical Society

Robert Oppenheimer

When Robert was 8 years old, his brother, Frank Friedman, was born. The household of their childhood included Grandmother Friedman and usually two servants. The boys grew up in a large apartment overlooking the Hudson River. They lived in a subdued, tasteful atmosphere of culture and affluence. Although both parents were Jewish, they were not actively affiliated with a temple. They belonged to the Ethical Cultural Society, founded by another German immigrant, Felix Adler, whose educational philosophy was centered in the cult of the individual. Robert entered the second grade at the Ethical Culture School in September 1911; he graduated from the high school division ten years later.

Robert kept very much to himself. He was a brilliant student with a voracious appetite for learning and great facility for languages. With the exception of sailing, he had no interest in sports. His family spent their summers at Bay Shore on the south coast of Long Island. Robert's father gave him a sailboat in which he and Frank endlessly sailed the Great South Bay. Over time, Robert became an expert yachtsman and as a teenager developed a taste for danger.

In his last year at Ethical Culture, Robert met Francis Fergusson from Albuquerque, New Mexico. They became great friends, and both expected to enter Harvard together the following autumn. Robert returned from a trip to Europe that summer, seriously ill with what was apparently a case of trench dysentery. He did not enter Harvard but spent the school year recuperating at home. By spring he was totally bored with his limited existence, and his father asked Herbert Smith, his high school English teacher, to take him west to the mountains to recuperate. They visited Francis and his family in Albuquerque.

The two men spent weeks roaming the mountains of Colorado and New Mexico on horseback, camping out at night or staying at guest ranches. One of those ranches was Los Piños near Cowles, New Mexico, a small community twenty miles up the Pecos Valley in the Sangre de Cristo Mountains northeast of Santa Fe. The ranch was run by the 28-year-old, beautiful, newly married Katherine Chaves Page. She was from an old aristocratic family of noble Spanish origin. Under her tutelage, Robert became an enthusiastic and expert horseman. One of his favorite rides was across the Rio Grande to the Los Alamos Ranch School on the Pajarito Plateau in the Jemez Mountains. Twenty years later, the memory of that rewarding experience would determine the location of a top-secret wartime laboratory.

The freedom and openness of his first western experience, the grandeur of the mountains, and the kindnesses of Katherine Page left an indelible impression on this frail young man from New York. He formed a deep attachment to the people and places of northern New Mexico and returned to those mountains time and time again in the succeeding two decades. He and Katherine maintained a warm friendship that lasted until her death in 1961.

Robert entered Harvard College as a freshman in September 1922. In three years he completed four years' work and graduated in 1925, summa cum laude, with an A.B. degree in chemistry.

Toward the end of his undergraduate studies, he began attending a course in advanced thermodynamics given by Percy Bridgman, a distinguished experimental physicist. Robert worked on a research project with Bridgman and decided to begin his postgraduate work in physics at the Cavendish Laboratory in Cambridge, England. The Cavendish was one of the great international centers in physics, a mecca for the most brilliant students and researchers in the field.

To his chagrin, Robert discovered that his background in experimental physics and mathematics was not sufficient for the required laboratory work. Despite his frustration with this inadequacy, he began to develop his own inclination for physics. In the spring of that difficult year, Robert met Max Born, director of the Institute of Theoretical Physics at the University of Göttingen in Germany. Born invited him to continue his work there. Accepting Born's offer put Robert in the midst of an extraordinary group of professors, postdoctoral fellows, and students who were deep in the application of the new quantum mechanics. Like Cambridge, Göttingen was one of the great European centers of physics. While Cambridge had a tradition of outstanding experimental work, Göttingen was above all a theoretical center. Robert worked with great intensity and earned a Ph.D. in one year.

In the 1927-28 year, he had a National Research Council postdoctoral fellowship at Harvard and the California Institute of Technology (Caltech) in Pasadena. By then he had made significant contributions to the development of the new quantum mechanics and was avidly recruited for university positions. From a wide range of options (ten offers from American universities, two from abroad), Robert accepted an assistant professorship at the University of California at Berkeley.

In the summer of 1928, he was diagnosed with tuberculosis and went with his 17-year-old brother, Frank, to the mountains of New Mexico to rest and recover. Robert contacted Katherine Page, who took him to visit a rustic log cabin that was available to rent. The building sat on top of a meadow with a magnificent view out across the Sangre de Cristo Mountains. It was an ideal spot. He leased it immediately and purchased it years later. He gave the place the nickname of Perro Caliente, Spanish for "hot dog." The cabin, which he referred to as "the ranch," came to be a place of comfort and renewal for him and his friends and family over the next forty years. At the end of that summer, a medical examination showed that Robert's "TB" had been held in check. There may be some doubt as to whether or not his respiratory problem was properly diagnosed as he was fit to leave for Europe in early October. He returned to Europe to spend another year at the leading centers of theoretical physics.

Robert arrived at the University of California in Berkeley in the fall of 1929. He arranged an unusual double teaching schedule with Berkeley and Caltech. For several years he taught the fall term at Berkeley and went to Pasadena after Christmas for the spring semester. Robert was not an instant success as a teacher. Students complained that he went too fast, mumbled, and was impossible to follow. Over time he dropped the pace of his delivery, took care to clarify the links between his ideas, and became an excellent lecturer. Oppenheimer attracted a small group of some of the country's brightest physics students and postdoctoral fellows. Many followed him from Berkeley to Pasadena and some to Perro Caliente where he and Frank spent their summers in the 1930s.

In 1936 Robert began to develop a new social and political consciousness that was nurtured by the spread of fascism abroad and the Great Depression at home. Both touched him directly. Deeply troubled by the growing anti-Semitism in Germany, he helped his German relatives emigrate to the United States. The devastating effects of the Depression curtailed the employment opportunities of his graduate students. The only positions available to many of them completely undervalued their training; for others there were no jobs.

For a man of his brilliance and sophistication, Robert was unusually impressionable and leaned heavily on other people to shape his political activism. Among his "teachers," none was closer or more important to him than Jean Tatlock, daughter of a noted professor of English at Berkeley. The couple met in the spring of 1936 when she was studying psychiatry at Stanford Medical School. She confided in him about her sporadic membership in the Communist Party. By fall he was courting her. They grew very close and twice thought of themselves as engaged. Their intense on-again, off-again relationship lasted until the late 1930s.

Oppenheimer spent much of the summer of 1940 at Perro Caliente with Frank, his wife, Jackie, and their baby daughter. Katherine Puening Harrison, wife of Stewart Harrison, an English physician engaged in cancer research at Caltech, was among the guests. Over the previous year Robert and Katherine Harrison, always known as Kitty, had developed a deep fondness for each other. Before her marriage to Harrison, Kitty had been the wife of Joe Dallet, a Communist Party organizer who was killed fighting in the Spanish Civil War in 1937. During that liaison, Kitty was also a Communist Party member, although she lacked enthusiasm for the cause. Toward the end of 1938 she married Stewart Harrison, whom she had known in England a few years earlier. Shortly thereafter he had returned to Pasadena, and Kitty followed him there after she received her bachelor's degree in biology from the University of Pennsylvania in June 1939.

Before the first anniversary of her marriage to Harrison, Kitty and Robert Oppenheimer had fallen in love. She filed for a Nevada divorce in the autumn of 1940, and on November 1 she and Oppenheimer were married there. They proceeded to Berkeley where they lived first in Robert's apartment on Shasta Road, then at 10 Kenilworth Court until August 1941 when they bought a house, 1 Eagle

Hill, in the Berkeley hills. Their first child, Peter, was born in May 1941.[3]

Robert had broken off his relationship with Jean Tatlock when he met Kitty, but in June 1943, shortly after he had assumed his duties as director of the Manhattan Project in Los Alamos, Jean sent word that she wanted to see him. At the time, she was undergoing psychiatric treatment and was very unhappy. Feeling guilty that he had not seen her before he left for New Mexico, Robert yielded to her wishes. He went to her home on Telegraph Hill and, unaware that he was under surveillance, spent the night. The following morning Jean drove him to the airport, and he never saw her again. Seven months later, in January 1944, she committed suicide. Oppenheimer's visit to Jean Tatlock, no matter how humane his intention, came to have a devastating effect on his career a decade later.

The "business" that took him to San Francisco and filled his life at that point was the recruitment of scientists and staff for the Manhattan Project. Three months earlier he had hired Dorothy McKibbin to serve as the "front man" for that operation in Santa Fe. Dorothy has been described as one of Oppenheimer's "inspired appointments."[4] She had lived in Santa Fe for eleven years before she met Robert in the lobby of La Fonda. From her work at the Spanish and Indian Trading Company, her experience building a house in Santa Fe, and her wide association with leaders of the arts community, she knew what was happening in town, and she knew how to get things done.

Dorothy was a resourceful woman with a strong sense of responsibility for her young son, who was 12 when his mother changed jobs. She also had an independent spirit and affinity for taking risks, embodied in her decision to move to Santa Fe despite family pressure to stay in Kansas City. Yet there was nothing wild or flamboyant in her character.

Dorothy and Robert shared similarities in their backgrounds.

Los Alamos Historical Society

Dorothy saw in Robert the magnetism she loved in Joe McKibbin.

Educated in private high schools and highly selective colleges—Smith and Harvard—each was from a wealthy family. Although Kansas City did not offer the cultural advantages of New York City, Dorothy had traveled widely throughout the world as a young woman, had married a charming, sophisticated man who was as comfortable in the Ivy Club at Princeton as in the open spaces of New Mexico. Both Dorothy and Robert had first come to New Mexico for reasons of health, and each had fallen in love with the land of enchantment. Both found a way to return. Although no match for Robert's intellectual brilliance, Dorothy was confident and secure wherever she found herself.

Dorothy had been without Joe for twelve years when she was introduced to Oppenheimer. Married only four years, Joe and Dorothy were at the beginning of their life together, still in the "honeymoon phase," when Joe died. Dorothy's memories of him were strong and loving. Clearly he was the great love of her life and always remained so. Yet when Dorothy saw Robert Oppenheimer, it is probable that she saw in him the qualities that she loved in Joe McKibbin. Her instantaneous response describes falling in love at first sight. "I never met a person with a magnetism that hit you so fast and so completely as his did.... I just wanted to be allied and have something to do with a person of such vitality and radiant force. That was for me."[5] It was as though she were struck by lightning.

Separated by age (he was 38; she 46), intellectual prowess and scientific background, there was, nevertheless, a strong bond between them from that first meeting. They became great friends who quite simply adored each other throughout their lives. David Hawkins, biographer of the Manhattan Project, summed up their relationship when he said, "Dorothy loved Robert Oppenheimer. He was her special one, and she, his."[6]

Part Three
GATEKEEPER TO LOS ALAMOS

Chapter 9

ESTABLISHING THE MANHATTAN PROJECT

Adolf Hitler came to power in Germany on January 30, 1933. Shortly thereafter, he began his systematic persecution of European Jews. The Third Reich issued its first anti-Jewish ordinance on April 7, proclaiming that civil servants of non-Aryan descent must retire. Since universities were state institutions and members of their faculties were civil servants, the new law abruptly robbed Germany of one quarter of its physicists. There was no work for them. To survive they had to emigrate. Colleagues in other countries moved quickly to aid the displaced scholars.

Meanwhile, scientific work in nuclear fission was going forward at the Kaiser Wilhelm Institute of Chemistry in Berlin. In 1938, drawing on work done in Paris by Irene and Frederic Joliot-Curie, Otto Hahn, a German chemist, and his assistant, Fritz Strassmann, bombarded uranium with neutrons and got a puzzling outcome. Hahn sent a letter outlining these experimental results to his former scientific collaborator, Lise Meitner, an Austrian physicist who had fled Nazi Germany and taken refuge in Stockholm. On her first Christmas in exile, she and her nephew, Otto Frisch, also a physicist, who had gone to

Denmark to escape Hitler's race laws, met in the Swedish village of Kungälv. She showed him Hahn's letter. As they walked up and down along the North River in the Christmas Eve snow, Meitner and Frisch analyzed Hahn's work and concluded that he and Strassman had split the uranium nucleus.

In July 1939, Leo Szilard, a Hungarian physicist familiar with the above results, conferred with Eugene Wigner, a Hungarian colleague, and Albert Einstein at Einstein's summer home on Long Island. Szilard, who did not drive a car, had enlisted the young Edward Teller, another Hungarian physicist who would become known as the "father of the hydrogen bomb," to drive them to this meeting. The scientists prepared a letter signed by Einstein to alert President Roosevelt to the importance of uranium fission and the likelihood that a nuclear chain reaction could lead to the construction of an atomic bomb. They warned that Germany might already be working on an atomic weapon.

By the time the letter was delivered on October 11, 1939, World War II had begun. Germany had invaded Poland; Britain and France had declared war on Germany. It was not until December 6, 1941, however, the day before Pearl Harbor and three years after the discovery of atomic fission, that the decision was made to support an all-out U.S. effort in atomic energy research. Until that time, virtually all laboratory research had been focused on achieving a controlled chain reaction by using U-235, a rare isotope of uranium. Scientists came to realize that unless unprecedented quantities of U-235 could be produced in a much purer state, a U-235 chain reaction would be impossible.

Researchers at the Metallurgical Laboratory at the University of Chicago began an intensive program of plutonium research. Their purpose, under the direction of Nobel laureate Arthur H. Compton, was to develop the knowledge needed to design, build, and operate a facility for the conversion of uranium into plutonium. In the summer of 1942,

Compton asked Robert Oppenheimer to organize a group of theoretical physicists to investigate whether, if reasonably pure fissionable material were available, an explosive could be made, and if so, how.

While Oppenheimer was meeting in Berkeley, the Manhattan Engineer District (MED) was formed to carry out the Army's responsibilities in the development of an atomic weapon. The new district took its name from New York City, briefly the site of the MED headquarters. In mid-September 1942, Col. Leslie R. Groves, a West Point graduate and a career officer who had studied engineering at Massachusetts Institute of Technology, was chosen to lead the new district and promoted to brigadier general. He was completing construction of the Pentagon and hoping to go overseas. At the time of his appointment, "There was barely enough plutonium in the world to cover the head of a pin and very little uranium 235, the only elements that could fuel an atomic bomb."[1]

On December 2, 1942, under an abandoned football stadium at the University of Chicago, the first controlled chain reaction was achieved under the direction of Enrico Fermi. As Groves learned more about the project, he understood the urgent need to build a laboratory and develop an actual bomb. He knew he needed to find a laboratory director who would command the respect of the scientists, have the intellect and imagination to grasp and solve all aspects of the scientific problems, and display the leadership ability to mold a group of strong-willed individuals into working teams. At the same time, this civilian director also needed to work within the confines of a military installation under the tightest security conditions.

On October 8, 1942, Groves went to the University of California at Berkeley where he had his first meeting with Robert Oppenheimer. They discussed the results of his summer study and the methods by which he had reached his conclusions. Groves asked him to come to Washington where they discussed what would be needed to develop an atomic bomb. Oppenheimer was perceived as knowing everything that was then known about "atomic science." However, he was not a natural first choice to direct the laboratory.

"My own feeling," wrote General Groves, "was that he was well qualified to handle the theoretical aspects of the work, but how he would do on the practical experimentation, or how he would handle the administrative responsibilities, I had no idea. I knew, of course, that he was a man of tremendous intellectual capacity, that he had a brilliant background in theoretical physics, and that he was well respected in the academic world."[2]

In addition to Oppenheimer's lack of administrative experience, he was not a Nobel Prize winner. Groves worried that Oppenheimer would lack prestige among his fellow scientists, most of whom felt that the laboratory director should be a Nobel laureate. Within a few weeks, however, it became apparent that there was no better man available. With full knowledge of Oppenheimer's background, including his liaison with Jean Tatlock and his brother's and wife's memberships in the Communist Party, Groves felt that his potential value outweighed any possible security risk. He asked Oppenheimer to take the job.

Finding a site for the secret laboratory, dubbed Project Y, was the immediate top priority for Groves and Oppenheimer. They assigned the task of identifying possible locations to Major John Dudley. He was told to look for an inland location free from the threat of invasion with a temperate climate suitable for year-round outdoor work. For safety and security reasons, the laboratory needed to be in a sparsely populated area, yet accessible by road and train, with enough timber-free land to build a new community. In order to attract a group of highly talented scientists, it was necessary that the laboratory be in a desirable setting with satisfactory working and living conditions.[3]

After a lengthy search, the area around Albuquerque, New Mexico, appeared to meet their needs. The location was free of the threat of attack by Japan's military along the West Coast. Rail service was available between Albuquerque and Chicago, providing access to Los Angeles, San Francisco, and Washington, D.C. All TWA flights to and from both the East and West coasts stopped there for refueling. The climate was excellent for their purposes.

Jemez Springs, deep in the mountains about sixty-seven miles north of Albuquerque, was the first site recommended to them. Groves and Oppenheimer inspected the area, which was hemmed in by cliffs on two sides. The rock faces created natural observation points almost impossible to patrol, and there was little room for expansion should the laboratory grow beyond original expectations. They declared it unsatisfactory.

Oppenheimer then suggested that they drive over the mountains toward Santa Fe to look at the property of Los Alamos Ranch School, located at 7,200 feet on the Pajarito Plateau between the Jemez and the Sangre de Cristo mountain ranges. Over the years he had visited the school on horseback pack trips into the area.

As a possible site for the development of an atomic bomb, the Pajarito Plateau had a singularly appropriate geological history. It was formed by a huge explosion—the eruption of the Jemez volcano. The caldera and the surrounding peaks were created by a series of upheavals dating back perhaps ten or more million years. The volcanic ash from these eruptions hardened into a soft rock called tuff that dominates the area.

Ancestral Puebloans carved homes in the cliffs of Frijoles Canyon, named for the beans grown along the creek, which flows year-round southeast from the Jemez Mountains to the Rio Grande. The canyon is in Bandelier National Monument, about six miles south of Los Alamos as the crow flies, and includes more than 23,000 acres of designated wilderness. Between A.D. 1150 and the time of the Spanish occupation in 1598, thousands of Indians evidently lived and died on the Pajarito Plateau.They farmed the valleys by day, retreating at night to the relative security of their cliff dwellings. Their descendants probably lived in the Cochiti and San Ildefonso pueblos a few miles east on the Rio Grande. The remains of the ancient villages can be seen today for more than a mile along the talus slopes of Frijoles Canyon, which is also home to the ruins of Tyuonyi, a circular two-story pueblo built in the 13th century at the bottom of the canyon.

Los Alamos Ranch School took its name from the nearby Los Alamos Canyon. In Spanish, Los Alamos means "the poplars, the cottonwoods." A unique preparatory school for teen-age boys, the Ranch School was the culmination of the lifelong dream held by Ashley Pond Jr., who started the school in 1917. Pond, who had grown up in Detroit, Michigan, was plagued with constant colds and bronchitis. During the Spanish-American War, he enlisted with Teddy Roosevelt's Rough Riders, but suffered a life-threatening siege of typhoid fever before he saw active duty. Like Oppenheimer, he had been sent west by his father to recover.

Pond dreamt of founding a school "where a healthful, rugged, outdoor-oriented education would prepare city-bred boys for college and for life."[4] He chose A.J. Connell, an enthusiastic outdoorsman and forest ranger in the nearby Santa Fe National Forest, to direct the school.

Connell organized it on the model of the Boy Scouts of America. The required daily school unform was khaki shorts worn with a khaki or wool flannel shirt and a bright bandana around the neck.The outfit was topped by a Dakota Stetson.[5] Academic college preparatory courses filled the morning hours. The main meal of the day was served at 1:20, followed by a rest period. Afternoon activities included work for the community on Mondays when the boys were divided into crews that built and cared for most of the athletic facilities and improved nearby forest and canyon trails. Games or horseback rides were the focus of other days. Each boy was assigned a horse to ride and groom. On weekend camping trips, each boy carried his own cooking kit and learned camping skills that "were as much a part of the school curriculum as Latin and geometry."[6] Between 1917 and 1942 nearly five hundred boys between the ages of 12 and 18 attended the Ranch School.

When Groves, Oppenheimer, and their site planners drove into the school area, Groves sensed at once that this was the right place for the laboratory. It met their exact specifications. The land surrounding the school was national forest or private homesteads. The nearest town was sixteen to eighteen miles away, and there was plenty of room on the mesa to house the original estimate of thirty scientists and one hundred staff members needed for the project.

Groves decided to acquire the school and take charge of Bandelier National Monument, which was managed by the National Park Service. Closing access to Bandelier ruins, trails, and Frijoles Lodge was not a serious disruption. Due to bad weather, tire shortages, gas rationing, and poorly maintained, unpaved roads, few visitors had made their

Los Alamos Historical Society

The isolated Ranch School site offered plenty of room to house the scientists and staff originally expected for the Project.

way to Bandelier during the summer of 1942.[7]

On November 20 A.J. Connell was notified that the school would be surveyed by the Manhattan Engineer District. He agreed to cooperate with condemnation proceedings on the one condition that the students be permitted to finish the school year. On December 7, the first anniversary of Pearl Harbor, Connell received notice from Secretary of War Henry Stimson that the school was being acquired for military purposes. Christmas holidays were canceled, and a special schedule was set up to complete the year's program at midyear. The final diplomas were awarded on January 21, 1943; the school officially closed on February 8.

Weeks before the official take-over date, bulldozers and mechanical ditch diggers had moved in to tear up the frozen ground. Groves had by then convinced the University of California to serve as general contractor for the secret laboratory. With the site chosen and construction started, Oppenheimer began to recruit a staff. That was a tall order. He needed to convince the best available scientific minds to "work for a purpose he could not disclose, at a place he could not specify, for a period he could not predict."[8]

At that time, most of the country's scientists were fully engaged in the war effort. Furthermore, leading scientific researchers, as civilians, had complete freedom in their choice of jobs. Accustomed to living in cities or near large metropolitan areas, many were not inclined to move to a remote, sparsely populated area under military control. Regardless of the obstacles, Oppenheimer was able to assemble a staff of world-famous scientists and young leaders in atomic research. They recognized the importance of the project and were fascinated by the challenge it provided. "I joined enthusiastically," said Victor Weisskopf, an Austrian physicist trained at Göttingen, "because of many reasons. First, my friends and I were very much afraid that the Germans would get it [the atomic bomb] before the United States. Second...how could a young man of thirty-five years not join a project of this kind that was full of the best and greatest physicists?"[9]

Writing about the recruitment of scientists thirty years later, Dorothy added her own view of the world situation:

> There was another factor, one...the modern generation does not know, having not experienced it, and one...too many of those who lived through the 30s and 40s tend to forget, or to have diminished to near-forgetting. The world was in a war, a brutal, bitter, costly war, a world war. Hitler and his Nazi army were in control of all of Europe with the exception of England, fighting for its life, and Russia, which could not be depended upon and had even joined up with Hitler until he turned against her. Not only did the United States have Germany threatening on and across the Atlantic, Japan, without declaration of war, had destroyed the fleet of ships and planes that guarded our Pacific frontier. We were on our own, fighting a war on two separate continents. We had the moral support of England but she had no military support to share. As for Russia, she remained strictly detached until the final days [of the Pacific war] coming in just in time to demand her share of the loot.
>
> What is incredibly forgotten by today's critics of the work at Los Alamos is Hitler's boast that he would wipe out the Jews, which had already resulted in the merciless persecution and death of millions of innocent and helpless humans. Most of the great European scientists who came to Los Alamos and to other American laboratories had been fortunate enough to escape from the doom Hitler would have wreaked on them. All scientists at Los Alamos knew that the fission of the atom had been first achieved in Germany. Until after the war, they believed that the Germans were ahead of us in the potentiality of building a bomb, and unless we could be first to achieve it, the United States would be the next nation subjugated.[10]

By early spring of 1943, construction engineers, under Army supervision, had been working for almost three months, bulldozing volcanic rock that had lain undisturbed for some 25,000 years. Many of those workers were housed temporarily at Frijoles Lodge in Bandelier. Moving at great speed, using rough timber and building paper, they had almost completed a main building, five laboratories, a machine shop, a warehouse, a set of barracks, and barracks-like apartments. Ev-

Los Alamos Historical Society

By early spring of 1943, most of the Project buildings had been thrown together to produce a ramshacle community that officially did not "exist."

ery kind of prefabricated Army housing was arriving and being thrown up, producing a ramshackle town that resembled a frontier mining camp. The saving grace was the natural location: a mesa top surrounded by some of the most beautiful mountain country in the United States.

During that spring and summer, large Army trucks crawled up the hill to Los Alamos as young Indian boys from the nearby San Ildefonso Pueblo watched in wonder. At the same time, residents of Santa Fe began to observe an influx of strangers from all over the United States and parts of Europe. Hundreds of bewildered individuals converged on New Mexico to begin an extraordinary adventure.

Chapter 10

109 EAST PALACE AVENUE

On March 27, 1943, Dorothy Scarritt McKibbin began her work for the Santa Fe office of the Manhattan Project at 109 East Palace Avenue in the Trujillo Patio, part of an ancient Spanish hacienda, built in the late 1600s. The office was run by a small group of employ-

Los Alamos Historical Society

The patio entrance to Dorothy's office at 109 East Palace Avenue

ees that included Oppenheimer and his secretary, Priscilla Greene from Berkeley; Duane Muncy, the comptroller from the University of California; Dana Mitchell, a young chemistry professor from Columbia who handled the procurement of scientific supplies; Joe Stevenson, the housing director; and Dorothy. They worked out of five overcrowded offices in the old adobe house, heated by a fireplace in the corner of each room. Dorothy's salary was $150 per month.

On her first day of work, Dorothy asked Joe Stevenson,"What are my instructions and what is the agenda?" He replied, "Your instructions are never to ask for a name to be repeated and never to ask a question."[1] In fact, the name, "Los Alamos," was not spoken there; it was referred to as "The Hill." A small wooden sign on the outer adobe wall beside the gate spelled out "U.S. Eng." Since the board was not long enough for the full word, the last two letters of the abbreviation were on the line below, "rs."

"It is hard to describe what we did," Dorothy wrote. "If you took a kaleidoscope and twirled it around and sailed it through the air and looked at it, this is the way our activities were. Whatever had to be done, by Jove we had to do it, and took great delight in the attempt. There was never a dull moment, never, never, never. The office was a madhouse. It was bedlam. We worked six days a week, but even so, I could not wait to get back to work in the morning."[2]

Before she left for home each evening, Dorothy was required to burn every scrap of paper, every office note, every piece of carbon paper that turned up in the course of each day. The one permanent record she kept was a meticulously typed 3-inch by 5-inch card file recording the arrival, transfer, and departure date of every civilian who came to her office.

Army guards (G-2) crept around the offices and stood in the shadow of the old portal day and night. Dorothy felt well protected and observed, "You could always spot a G-2 man—they wore snap-brimmed hats, straw in summer, felt in winter. And they were the only men in Santa Fe dressed in three-piece suits and wingtip shoes."[3]

From the moment the office was established, top scientists from the United States and abroad arrived unannounced at the courtyard of 109. Uprooted from their university laboratories, they had sold or rented their homes, deceived friends and family about their whereabouts, and traveled across the United States to a secret world. Most had fought their way to Santa Fe under wartime circumstances. The era of general air travel had not yet arrived. Trains were slow and held up for troop movements. Food was scarce; connections were missed; baggage was lost. One wife wrote, "I felt akin to the pioneer women accompanying their husbands across the uncharted plains westward, alert to danger, resigned to the fact that they journeyed for weal or woe, into the Unknown."[4]

All civilians and a few military personnel came into the Manhattan Project through a wrought-iron gate leading to the thick-walled, weather-beaten, old Spanish building at 109 East Palace Avenue. The courtyard, where birds sang and built their nests, was bordered with small pink climbing roses and tall pink hollyhocks. Expecting anything and everything, the best and the worst, the travelers arrived sleepless, hungry, and confused.

Dorothy McKibbin, whose voice was quiet and manner unhurried, was the first contact for these bewildered and occasionally disillusioned individuals, some of whom had been led to believe they were going overseas. Weary travelers thought that they had "arrived" when they reached 109. Tired families with small babies came in and said they had sent their furniture there, but it didn't look like much of a home. Machinists dashed in and asked, "Where is the dance hall?" Others said, "... I think I will leave my suitcase down here, I may not like it."[5]

One of the most immediate disappointments was the fact that Dorothy's office was not the end of the journey. Their real destination

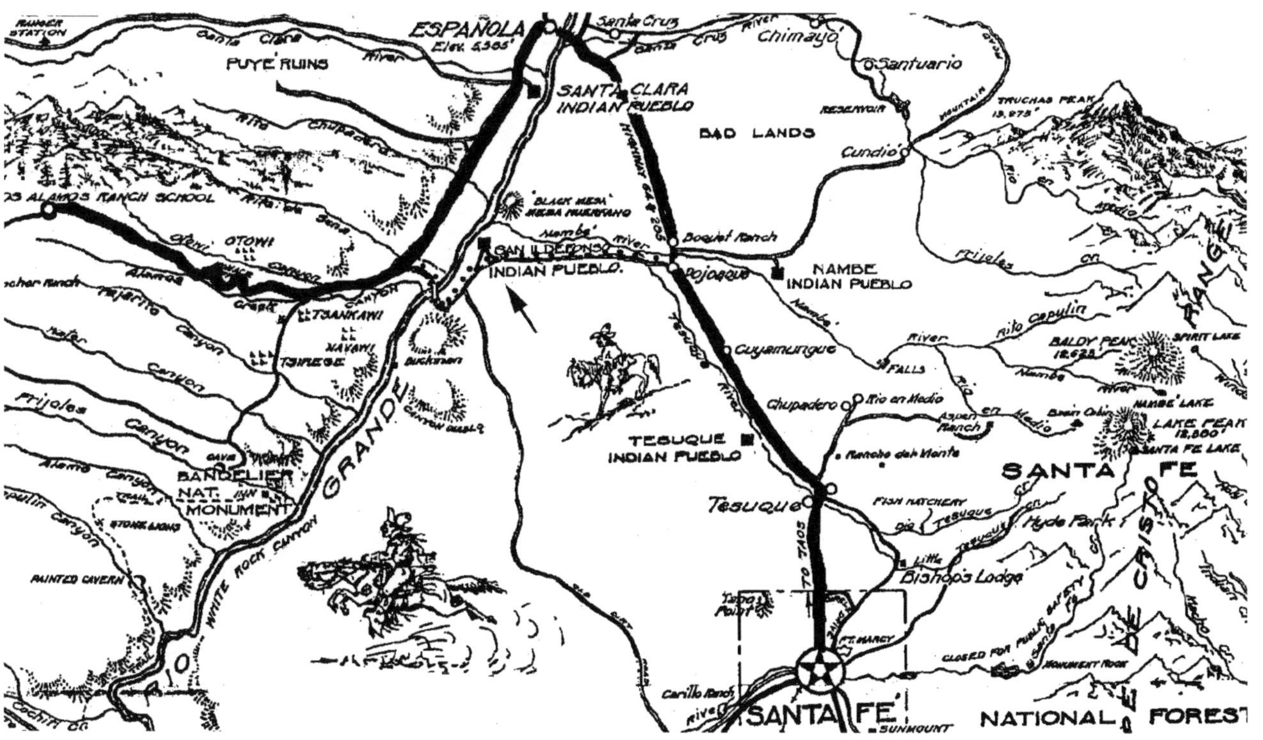

This portion of a 1936 road map, possibly a copy of the map Dorothy distributed to new arrivals, shows the forty-five-mile route to Los Alamos. The arrow indicates the road across Otowi Bridge that could not be used.

Los Alamos Historical Society

The winding dirt road to Los Alamos was improved later. Both the old (center) and new routes are visible in this view.

was the Hill, which meant driving a tortuous dirt road, descending from Santa Fe into Tesuque, Nambe, and the Rio Grande valley, near the pueblos of Santa Clara and San Ildefonso, and then ascending the steep last ten miles to the top of the mesa. Dorothy handed each new arrival a yellow map inscribed with red pencil, marking every mile and every turn of the road but without noting the actual distance. Because the bridge over the Rio Grande at Otowi was too narrow and fragile to support heavy traffic, road transportation was routed through Española until a new bridge could be built. This added an extra ten miles to what would have been a difficult thirty-five-mile trip. When the newcomers reached the end of their mysterious drive, they found a shabby array of temporary buildings, scattered helter-skelter over the landscape.

In the course of one day, during those hectic early months, Dorothy would dispatch an average of sixty-five people to the Hill. She would arrange shipment for trucks of freight, including critical scientific equipment for the laboratory, vans of furniture, special orders for baby cribs, fresh flowers, hot rolls, and pumpernickel bread. She would handle more than one hundred telephone calls on the one erratic Forest Service line that had been chewed by squirrels and buffeted by storms. She issued dozens of passes, made out in triplicate. No one could go through the sentry gate at Los Alamos without a pass. Dorothy came to be known as the "gatekeeper to Los Alamos."

She cared for children, watched over pets, guarded bundles and briefcases. With her encyclopedic knowledge of the greater Santa Fe area, she was able to answer the needs of the newcomers no matter what the request: a new puppy or horse, thread of a special color, a goose for the Oppenheimers' Christmas dinner, a doctor who would perform an abortion. Dorothy made herself available to find anything that anybody wanted whenever they needed it.

She was some twenty years older than most of the incoming Los Alamos "recruits" and their wives. With considerable patience and kindness, Dorothy was a natural shock absorber to many of the lonely and disillusioned souls, cut off from their families and the outside world, who came to New Mexico at a time of national crisis. Dorothy knew first hand about illness and death and the problem of creating a new life in an area far removed from one's original roots. She became a quasi "mother superior" and guidance counselor for hundreds of young women and their children.

"All women brought their difficulties…to Dorothy," noted Laura Fermi, wife of Enrico Fermi. "Yes, she knew of a boys' camp. Yes, she could recommend a good eating place. Yes, she could arrange for a ride to the mesa later in the evening. Yes, she would try to get reservations at a good hotel in Albuquerque."[6] Dorothy had a doggedness about her that kept her at a job until it was done to perfection. Those on the Hill who encountered problems often spoke of "consulting the Oracle" when seeking her help.

"Working at 109 was more than just a job," Dorothy wrote. "We worked with pride. We sensed the excitement and suspense of the Project, for the intensity of the people coming through the office was contagious. It was an exciting experience. Our office served as the entrance to one of the most significant undertakings of the war or, indeed, of the twentieth century."[7]

The door at 109 East Palace was the approach to a strange new world in that still innocent year of 1943. It would be two more years before recognition would come that 109 was the entrance to the Atomic Age. And sixty years after those remarkable days of early Los Alamos, friends remember Dorothy for the warmth of her smile and the quiet reassurance she radiated through each crisis. A rare combination of gentility and fire, she was a powerful civilizing influence where, under the urgency of war, haste and expediency guided every task.

Courtesy Museum of New Mexico Neg. 30187

Dorothy demonstrates for photographers the busy life at 109.

Short-time visitors were put up in apartments in Fuller Lodge, the Ranch School's dining hall and infirmary.

Project administrators were assigned to the coveted Bathtub Row houses.

The school's Big House provided housing for Project bachelors.

Chapter 11

EARLY DAYS ON THE HILL

Housing was a major challenge in the opening preparations for the atomic laboratory. At first, before accommodations were ready on the Hill, Oppenheimer, his key personnel, and a handful of incoming scientists stayed in Santa Fe hotels. Fearing that too many strangers in the non-tourist season would give rise to speculation about their purpose in town, the number housed in Santa Fe was kept very small. In the same vein it was thought that too many assorted European accents would arouse concern about the presence of German spies. Using hotels also risked the possibility that some of the famous scientists might be recognized from pictures in national news magazines.

In the early spring of 1943, the school buildings on the grounds of the Ranch School provided lodging for some of the incoming scientists. The Big House, the original center of the school, housed bachelors. Scientists who came for brief consultations were put up in Fuller Lodge, the school's dining hall and infirmary, which had a few apartments on the third floor. There were a number of smaller cabins that had been the masters' houses. They became the quarters for top Project administrators. This group of buildings, the only houses in Los Alamos with bathtubs, quickly became known as "Bathtub Row." Since General Groves frowned on luxuries, only showers were installed in the small apartments and dormitories under construction.

Joe Stevenson, the housing director, lived on a small ranch in the Pojoaque valley, midway between Santa Fe and Los Alamos. He arranged housing for many of the scientists at four larger ranches nearby. Transportation employees often overlooked scientists living there and forgot to pick them up on their bus runs. A neglected scientist, usually in the midst of a laboratory experiment, would howl with anger over the Forest Service phone line to Dorothy, seeking her help. The local men hired to drive the Los Alamos route also could not understand why they had to make the round trip twice a day, and they didn't like meandering about and waiting for passengers. "The mañana spirit indigenous to northern New Mexico suffused the entire project," Dorothy noted.[1]

"There was an amateur clumsiness about the whole Los Alamos project from the opening of 109 through the testing of the atomic bomb and beyond.This quality may have been dangerous, and frequently was," she observed, "but there was something endearing about its lack of sophistication. Most of the men who came to the Hill were boys, brilliant boys but boys nonetheless."[2] Twenty-five was the average age. Duties and priorities had to be established while the work was getting done.

Everything that was used in Los Alamos was taken up the winding mesa road on wheels or by hand, from a fountain pen to a carton of milk, from parts of a cyclotron to great girders for a bridge. Edward Teller and his wife, Mici, shipped two items, they considered essential to their household: a Steinway grand piano and a new Bendix washing machine. Dorothy and the one or two secretaries who worked with her made out triplicate slips for every article that was sent up in trucks. In the early period, because commissaries had not yet been constructed, there was no way to preserve food or to prepare it on the Hill. Dorothy

McKibbin ordered box lunches each day from restaurants in Santa Fe. She shifted from one restaurant to another to keep the owners from questioning why there were such large picnic orders when it wasn't yet picnic season.

Joe Stevenson ransacked Santa Fe and the surrounding countryside looking for any vehicle that would run. The transportation fleet consisted of battered station wagons, rusty sedans, dilapidated trucks and a few antediluvian buses. Few scientists brought their cars to the secret project. Basically they had no idea whether or not they could use them in the "wilderness." Gas rationing was in effect, and with most scientists coming from the East or West coasts, it was difficult if not impossible to secure enough fuel to make the long trip to New Mexico.

By the time the office at 109 was opened, the laboratories on the Hill were nearly ready for use. The structures, both below and above ground, had been contracted as piece work; no one builder knew the entire construction plan. The scientists alone knew the exact purpose of each building. People in Santa Fe joked about what they thought was taking place on the Hill. They called it a home for pregnant Wacs or a manufacturing plant for windshield wipers for submarines. Local residents buttonholed workers from 109 and asked, "What's going on up there?" The standard evasive reply was, "Don't you know there's a war going on?" The local newspaper, the *New Mexican,* instructed its staff not to go into the East Palace office and ask questions because they would not be told anything. Shopkeepers in Santa Fe frequently called Dorothy and said, "There is a strange person in here. I think he is lost, and he does not know how to tell me where he is going." Dorothy would reply, "Say no more, send him right over."[3]

The office at 109 East Palace Avenue was the center of operations for Project Y of the Manhattan Engineer District until early May when Oppenheimer moved his staff to the Los Alamos site. Dorothy received three separate offers to move with them. The alternative for her was to remain in charge of what would be left of the 109 operation. Dorothy knew the excitement would be on the Hill, whatever that undertaking was all about. (She later admitted it took her about a year to figure out the purpose of the Manhattan Project.) However, a move there would mean living in temporary quarters in Los Alamos, leaving her precious home, and separating from her wide circle of Santa Fe friends and activities. Above all, she worried about what the change would mean for Kevin. He would have to leave his school, his friends, his dogs, cats, and chickens, and his pony as well as an assortment of horny toads, lizards, and snakes, and his infirmary for injured birds and animals.

The offers were tempting. In her usual thoughtful manner, she gave them serious consideration. Wisely, Dorothy decided to remain at 109 where she was in charge of the office with one or two secretaries to assist her. On the Hill, she would have been one more cog in the wheel of administration. She prized her independence and the unique role she played in the secret enterprise, and she loved to have her presence felt. The world revolved around her in Santa Fe.

Once she had decided to stay at 109, Dorothy calmly balanced the hectic pace as "den mother" to the builders of an atomic bomb and mother to a teen-age boy. She was in daily telephone contact with Priscilla Greene (soon to be Priscilla Duffield), Oppenheimer's secretary, and she went up to the Hill for staff meetings, making the trip several times a week and sometimes twice a day. Often Kevin went with her. He loved to go to the PX where he could get large Hershey chocolate bars, a rare luxury in Santa Fe during the war. Often she would drop him off in the canyon area around the Tsankawi Ruins where he explored the caves looking for Indian artifacts and petroglyphs. Dorothy's lack of fear in leaving him alone in that wild country attests to her trust in him. Lifelong, Kevin would enjoy his own company and be comfortable in the natural world.

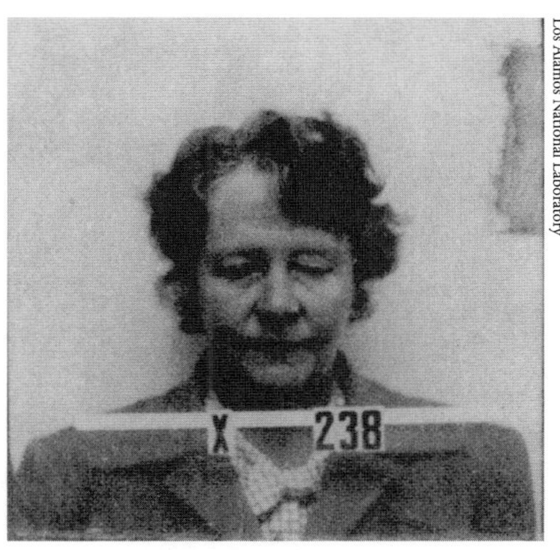

Los Alamos National Laboratory

Dorothy's early Q badge photo

In recognition of her position on the Project, Dorothy held a Q badge, the highest security ranking outside of Oppenheimer and the top scientists. Her home became a "safe house" where the scientists could remain over night when they needed to catch an early train in the morning or arrived too late in the day to continue up to the Hill. Top secret meetings and small dinner parties were often held there. She loved the evenings alone with Robert Oppenheimer when he would make "the best dry martinis you ever had," and she would cook their ritual dinner of steak and fresh asparagus.[4]

The house was often full of guests. Sometimes Kevin would come home to find a note on the kitchen table that said, "Grab a sleeping bag and find a place to park it." Kevin enjoyed meeting the scientists and was intrigued by how "normal" they seemed. When they were around the house, they did not "act like Ph.D.s" but took an interest in the things he was doing. "I never questioned what was going on, I just thought all those smart people who overflowed our house was neat."[5]

One of Kevin's prize recollections involves Edwin McMillan, a Nobel laureate and the co-discoverer of plutonium. "Ed got into Santa Fe late one night so he had to stay at the house until a bus was available at daybreak. I had a '27 Chevy that had a problem, and the next morning I was telling Ed about it, and soon we were both digging around under the hood. That's where my mother found us at noon after the lab had called, urgently searching for the scientist who had missed his crucial appointment."[6]

Laura Gilpin photo, 1948

The patio of Dorothy's home was the site of many wedding receptions for Los Alamos couples.

In the early days of the Project, there was no chapel on the Hill. Dorothy opened her home to young Los Alamos couples for their weddings. With its "carved Spanish doors, antique furniture, and windows overlooking the lights of the city," Dorothy's house was a romantic setting.[7] The weddings were small affairs, often with an older scientist giving the bride away. Security precluded having family and friends from home. Dorothy arranged for a minister or judge who would agree to perform the ceremony without divulging the full name of the bride and groom, using only their first names. All other arrangements—food, drink, decorations, guest list—were up to the young couple. If the weather was fair, the reception could be held outside on the U-shaped patio. The champagne was passed around sedately on the back of Monica Wells, a 100-year-old turtle that had belonged to Cady Wells and was part of the McKibbin menage. When a guest would reach for a glass, Monica would stop with dignity and poise, let them remove the glass, and then plod on to deliver more.

The first to wed there was Priscilla Greene, Oppenheimer's secretary, who married the chemist Robert Duffield on September 5, 1943. As was common in wartime, their courtship was a short one, not unlike that of shipboard romances, when couples marry after a brief period of acquaintance. Priscilla recalled, "I was in one dorm, and Duff, in another. The summer passed. In August, Duff and I sort of started going out with each other. Sometime in the middle of that month we decided to get married in September."[8] There were about twenty friends there, and the ladies all wore hats. It was a secure affair, with a military guard in full battle dress on the road in front of Dorothy's house. Oppenheimer was to serve as "father of the bride," but at the last moment he received a summons to meet with security officials in Cheyenne, Wyoming. He asked Priscilla to drive him as far as Santa Fe so that they could talk privately. She was touched by his concern and the fatherly advice he dispensed. Over time there were about thirty weddings at Dorothy's house, including those of Peter Oppenheimer, Robert and Kitty's son, and her granddaughter, Karen.

In the late spring of 1943, Dorothy was called to the Hill to meet with several assistants to the laboratory director. As usual, there was a housing shortage, and she was asked to open Frijoles Lodge in Bandelier National Monument and prepare it for the arrival of one hundred expected guests. She had five days to get it ready and then would be expected to manage it for the summer. Never having run a hotel, Dorothy was hesitant to accept this new assignment. Among other things, she wanted to make certain that the Santa Fe office would remain open while she was in Bandelier and that Kevin could enter the Los Alamos school if she needed to stay beyond the summer months. While she was thinking out loud about such matters, Oppenheimer opened the door of his inner office, stuck his head out, and said, "Dorothy, I wish you would do it."[9] And once again succumbing to his charm, she took the job. Oppenheimer knew that Dorothy could make any newcomer feel welcome anywhere in the world.

Newcomers were one thing, but "old timers" were another. She may also have been reluctant to dislodge Evelyn Cecil Frey who had been the undisputed mistress of Frijoles Canyon for eighteen years. Dorothy was astute enough to understand that there was tension between Mrs. Frey and those she considered military and civilian interlopers.

"Mrs. Frey" as she chose to be known, came into Frijoles Canyon with her husband, George, and their 10-month-old son in May 1925. They held a ninety-nine-year Forest Service lease for a small guest ranch there and worked tirelessly to make ends meet under primitive living conditions. They attempted to be self-sufficient by planting a new orchard and extensive gardens and keeping cattle, pigs, and chickens. George, a skilled mechanic, installed a cable system to bring down supplies from the top of the cliff. Mrs. Frey, the driving force behind the whole venture, took on the domestic chores of the ranch including making curtains for the windows and managing both the cabins and the lodge. Self-taught but widely read in archaeology and ethnology, she also conducted tours around the Indian ruins for her guests who arrived by burro down a steep switchback trail.[10]

In 1932 the National Park Service took over Bandelier National Monument. The Civilian Conservation Corps (CCC) and the Civil Works Authority (CWA) moved in to "modernize" the area and make it "an entry point for visitors coming to southwestern areas."[11] This modernization included the first road into the canyon, an administration/museum building, a swimming pool, a new lodge, and a parking area. The brick structures were made of tuff, "compacted volcanic ash quarried on the mesa top just outside the northern park boundary."[12]

Mrs. Frey, whose husband had left her in 1935, formally took possession of what were now considered "concessions" and moved into the new lodge in May 1939. Abandoning a simple existence that had meant so much to her was difficult. Guests at the old lodge usually sought isolation and solitude; the new facility offered a fine hotel with occasional entertainments. New expectations created a different atmosphere and the need for a larger staff.[13] She was confronted by even greater displacement early in 1943, when both Groves and Oppenheimer visited her and announced the closing of Frijoles Lodge as part of a clandestine government project.

Mrs. Frey was not in Bandelier when Oppenheimer asked Dorothy to reopen the lodge and prepare for a large influx of visitors. The "lady of the canyon" was visiting friends in New York and had tickets for several Broadway shows. Nevertheless, she was hustled aboard an airplane and, in the company of a number of Canadian military officers, flown to Albuquerque. She was met at the airport by a private car and rushed to Frijoles where she was instructed to inventory everything in the lodge and sign over the "right-of-entry" to the Army, effective June 3, 1943.[14] Mrs. Frey was deeply upset about having a large number of people move into the canyon, and she clearly had every right to be troubled. The previous spring, construction workers living in Frijoles Lodge while building the technical area at Los Alamos "trashed" their housing and left the facilities in shambles.

"[The contractors] were rather devastating in their hurry to get the buildings up....They also tried to bulldoze some trees...disrupting a lot of the ancient plantings and [the] charm of the place," Dorothy wrote. "I went in there cold, completely innocent of any ill will toward the [Manhattan] Project...."[15]

For two months beginning in early June, Dorothy left an assistant in charge of the Santa Fe office while she and Kevin moved to Bandelier where they were housed in adjoining cabins. For 12-year-old Kevin, who was fascinated by military equipment and ancient Indian sites, it was a magical time. There were no tourists in Frijoles Canyon, and he had the run of the whole place.

Dorothy, who acted as a shield between Mrs. Frey and the Army, was given every kind of support she needed. The Army brought her a generator "strong enough to light the city of Chicago."[16] She was issued a station wagon "for official use only." It came with no tools so she asked the GIs in the motor pool to help her out. They were quick to "liberate jacks and all sorts of wrenches and things [the] car lacked, a screwdriver, spare tire, lug wrench, etc."[17] Five young women came from the San Ildefonso Pueblo to help her clean. And what a mess they found—dead rats in the flour bins and bedroom fireplaces thick with grease from inside barbecue suppers!

As it happened, the extent of the housing shortage had been miscalculated. Occupancy ran somewhat under the estimated number. Dorothy, with the help of a chef, used the time and space to offer a buffet lunch and supper on Sundays for the families from the Hill. "They enjoyed coming over very much. They came with fishing tackle and took wonderful walks around Frijoles to the Stone Lions and to the Rio Grande, and it was a very pleasant …relaxing experience for all of us."[18]

Chapter 12

THE LOS ALAMOS COMMUNITY

Los Alamos was a world unto itself, a unique and uneasy combination of military and civilian cultures. Isolated on the top of a mesa, it was a town with one mission: to work out the technical feasibility of building an atomic bomb. The estimated population as of January 1943 was approximately 1,500; by the end of 1944, it had reached 5,675. A sharp increase during 1945 raised that number to 8,200.[1]

The Army controlled the town; the laboratory was administered by the University of California under contract to the Army. From its inception, there was tension in the lab between the military and scientific approaches to problem solving. The goal of the scientists was to discover new information and explore new concepts through open investigation and the exchange of ideas. The Army, on the other hand, was committed to completing the project in total secrecy, guided by a tight compartmentalized hierarchy and the classification of information.

Life on the Hill was dominated by secrecy and security. Cordoned off by a high barbed-wire fence, patrolled on the outside by armed military guards, Los Alamos was the site for probably the most clandes-

Los Alamos Historical Society

Los Alamos Historical Society

Life on the Hill was dominated by security. Armed guards (top) patrolled outside the fence; residents had to show a pass leaving or entering the main gate (above).

tine undertaking of the 20th century. The scientists did not enjoy having to accept Army authority. In particular, they felt that security was too rigid. They also thought some of it was pretty silly. For example, they had to show a pass whenever they went in or out of the gate. Yet everyone, including the guards, knew there were great holes in the fence through which the average man could walk without stooping. The children particularly enjoyed baffling the guards at the gate by coming in when, according to the pass records, they had not been out.

Most of the scientists did not object to the confinement, at least not loudly. Rather it was the wives, most of whom did not understand the importance and nature of the Project, who did the complaining. A much-quoted comment on the whole Manhattan Project came from General Groves as he watched the turmoil of construction and listened to the demands of the scientists and their wives. "At great expense," he said, "we have gathered here the largest collection of crackpots ever seen."[2]

The Los Alamos community was an unusual collective enterprise. There was no unemployment, no rich or poor, no jails. Every head of household had a job and a place to live. Rent was determined by the Army, based on one's salary, not on rank or size of house. In 1943, those earning less than $2,600 a year paid $17 a month in rent; those who earned $3,400-3,800, $34 a month; over, $6,000, $67 a month. Utilities for the apartments were $10 to $13 per month, according to the space occupied.[3]

The rent system was developed to compensate for inequities in salary distribution. "Salaries were paid according to the last job held. Young men from lucrative jobs in industry hired for routine work on the Project were often paid more than senior university professors charged with responsibility for building the bomb. Young scientists without Ph.D.s often contributed important ideas but were paid stipends no larger than meager fellowship grants."[4]

Laboratory members were not allowed personal contact with relatives or friends. Residents were authorized to travel no more than one hundred miles from Los Alamos. On occasion, special permission was granted to stay out overnight and go to Mesa Verde, Denver, the Carlsbad Caverns, or El Paso. Even when off the mesa, there could be no conversations with friends or strangers. It was common knowledge that travelers were being watched by the Army G-2 (military intelligence) and the FBI.

Visits to Santa Fe were restricted to one per month. They were high points in the intense lives of women on the Hill. "Over a period of weeks, your list grew and grew," wrote Charlotte Serber, scientific librarian, whose husband, Robert Serber, was a group leader in the Theoretical Physics Division. "For some, the date for the trek was finally set by the state of their liquor supply; for others, by their supply of baby oil. When some such critical item hit bottom, your trip got classified ESSENTIAL. By this time your list was long enough to consume three shopping days."[5]

Lunch at La Fonda, a drink there when the shopping was done, and a visit with Dorothy McKibbin added to the pleasure of being off the mesa. Dorothy was a source of comfort and cheer to all who stopped by. It was on those visits that the women came to rely on Dorothy's wisdom and assuring manner. She became their friend and confidante. "109 East Palace and Dorothy, our only link with Santa Fe, became our secret club in the capital of New Mexico. There we could talk and make plans and have no fear of being overheard."[6]

In keeping with the need for anonymity, all incoming mail had to be addressed to P.O. Box 1663, Santa Fe, New Mexico. All outgoing mail was censored and had to be mailed unsealed. A favorite censor story concerned a chemist who wrote to a friend about the difficulties of his job. "I wish that I had spent more time on dramatics at school," he said. "I certainly have a bunch of prima donnas to manage here!" The censor returned the letter with a note pointing out that the writer was forbidden to reveal the nature of his work.[7]

Twice a day local military police transferred the mail from Santa Fe to Los Alamos. An MP and a mail clerk, both armed, drove to the Santa Fe post office to deliver outgoing mail and bring back incoming letters. Efforts were made to have all professional and academic mail sent to former addresses, usually universities, and hand forwarded by department secretaries. The purpose of this safeguard was to prevent enemy agents from realizing that America's leading scientific journals suddenly had hundreds of subscribers in northern New Mexico.[8]

Clothes were purchased from mail-order catalogs such as Sears Roebuck and Montgomery Ward. A story is told of one catalog delivery arriving with the following note: "You folks at Box 1663 sure do buy a lot!" Another letter sent to Box 1663, sternly stated, "We don't know what you are doing to our catalogues. We have sent more than 100 catalogues to this address and will send no more!"[9]

Famous names were disguised; occupations were not mentioned. Enrico Fermi became "Henry Farmer," Neils Bohr, "Nicholas Baker" or "Uncle Nick." The use of the word physicist was forbidden; everyone was an "engineer." The scientists, most with a Ph.D., were addressed as "mister," not "doctor." Telephone calls were monitored. Car titles and driver's licenses, insurance policies, food and gasoline ration books were issued to numbers rather than names. Birth certificates for those born in the Los Alamos hospital listed the place of birth as "P.O. Box 1663, Santa Fe, NM, Sandoval County, Rural." All deliveries were marked "U.S.E.D," standing for United States Engineer District. Albuquerque was the banking center for the Project; all banking was done by mail. There were no telephones in the houses, no mail man, no milk man, no paper boy. More important, residents of the Hill had no vote, a situation that rankled, especially as the presidential election of 1944 approached.

The architecture of Los Alamos was an odd combination of Army jerrybuilt, painted nondescript green, and log structures from the Ranch School. There were no garages, no sidewalks, no paved streets. Family housing consisted of two-story apartment buildings, housing four or eight families; duplexes; and prefabricated single-family houses. These units were named after the contractor who built them. The apart-

Los Alamos Historical Society

Project housing ranged from two-story apartment buildings, called Sundts, for four to eight families (above) to a variety prefabricated structures (below) brought in by the Army for the rapidly expanding population.

Los Alamos Historical Society

ment buildings, for example, were built by the M.M. Sundt Construction Company and were called Sundts. Prefabricated homes trucked in from the town of Hanford, Washington, were known as Hanfords.

A wooden water tower, the sole source of water for extinguish-

Los Alamos Historical Society

The Water Tower served as a landmark compass point from which all directions were given to the nameless streets.

ing fires, served as the landmark compass for the citizens of Los Alamos. Since the streets had no names, all directions were taken from there. Fire was a major worry. The walls of the houses were tissue paper thin, and the furnaces constantly overheated to temperatures of ninety to one hundred degrees. Often the heat was on in the daytime and off at night. The heat that poured out from grilled transoms left behind a black, sticky trail of soot and grease that covered the dishes and closets in the winter. In summer, dust poured through the doors and windows. The open transom also carried conversations from the furnace room, usually arguments in Spanish patois or voices raised in lusty song. The result of these intrusions was a peculiar lack of privacy.[10]

For each apartment and home, the military administration provided a modern electric refrigerator and, in what some considered its "typical perversity," a large, cumbersome, wood-coal burning stove for cooking food. These stoves, which were almost impossible to light at an altitude of 7,200 feet, became known as Black Beauties. On one occasion, a scientist's wife cornered General Groves about the problem of lighting the stove. Rashly he decided to show her how it could be done. An hour or more later, a flustered, sooty Groves achieved success, but the point had been made. In time, electric hot plates were issued to supplement the "monster." Since electric power was often in short supply, there were periods when the power was shut off or went off—regularly at 5:30 p.m. Frequently dinners were eaten by candlelight or not at all, if food could not be cooked.

The Jemez area is a dry land; drought, a common condition. Obtaining an adequate water supply to meet the needs of an expanding community was a constant challenge. Bulletins from the Army on how to conserve water were sent out regularly. Some of the many restrictions were: immediately report any leaking faucet; no watering of lawns or gardens; soap your body before entering the shower. In the case of the latter edict, the soaping was a disaster if the water did not come on, and it frequently did not!

Although the military administration of Los Alamos was the object of ongoing criticism, there were few complaints about the hospital and the doctors. Most medical and dental services as well as drugs were free. Los Alamos was a young community with a baby boom. Shirley Barnett, wife of Los Alamos pediatrician Henry Barnett, noted that "eighty babies were born during the first year, and about ten a month thereafter."[11] According to a widely told anecdote, Groves asked Oppenheimer to do something to curtail the high birth rate. Oppenheimer's reply, if any, is not known. But such a request would have put him in an awkward position as he was one of the proud fathers. His daughter, Toni, was born on December 7, 1944. The high birthrate—and Groves' displeasure—were celebrated in a jingle:

The General's in a stew
He trusted you and you.
He thought you'd be scientific
Instead you're just prolific
And what is he to do? [12]

Most of the women had jobs on the mesa. In many cases, the wives of young physicists and chemists had not planned to work when they came to Los Alamos. However, the urgent need for all hands, "trained or untrained," quickly brought them onto a payroll. The women took jobs as secretaries, typists, or clerks. Others served as technicians, teachers, librarians, or draftswomen. Only a few worked as scientists. Those who came with the idea of working part time, worked full time. Some intended to quit in a few months, but worked for one or two years. While the women were at work, their children were in school. There was a nursery school for two-to-five-year-olds and a twelve-grade school with sixteen teachers.

Working conditions included a forty-eight-hour work week, two weeks of paid vacation, sick leave, and one day off a month for a shopping trip to Santa Fe. There were six self-help laundries and a maid service to assist with household tasks. The demand for domestic help grew quickly and steadily as more and more women entered the work force. Eventually the Housing Office took on the task of recruiting women from the two nearby towns, small farms, and pueblos, within a fifteen-mile radius of Los Alamos. Occasionally, maids would come from as far away as the Taos Pueblo. Six days a week the Army sent buses down to the pueblos and Hispanic settlements to pick up the maids and bring them to the Hill. They were paid $3 for a full day's work; their work days were frequently shared with at least two families.

Despite the attempt to create a reasonable work schedule, human nature and cultural differences played havoc with such a plan. The maids developed preferences for certain families and often went where they pleased. They demonstrated an independence of attitude and action not usually associated with household help. Saints' Days and Feast Days, not celebrated on the Hill, were another challenge. It was difficult to learn in advance how many days a maid would be absent. Very few of the maids had worked outside their own homes. Things like vacuum cleaners defeated them, but they understood linoleum floors and loved to shine the Black Beauty stoves. They talked little and worked in an unhurried rhythm, a clear contrast to the urgency of the pace that dominated the work ethic on the Hill. Yet some became nannies and extended family members, and many made an indelible impression on the children of Los Alamos. Families visited the pueblos on Feast Days for the ancient Indian dances and ceremonies. Gifts were exchanged at Christmas, and many of the Hill residents had fine Indian pottery collections as a result of that holiday tradition.

Despite the difficulties of life on the mesa—the isolation, the security, and the intensity of working at fever pitch six days, and sometimes even nights, a week, there were many compensating factors. Unlike most wartime couples, husbands and wives were not separated from each other. Although few wives understood the magnitude of the scientific enterprise, the small family units were intact, and husbands did come home each night. There was a unity of purpose, a congeniality, among one of the most interesting groups of people ever assembled in the United States. They managed to adjust themselves to the "oddest conditions under which a community has ever been maintained and within these limits to lead reasonably normal, happy lives."[13]

Los Alamos was a fascinating international, intellectual community. It was not unusual to have five Nobel Prize winners in the same room at one time. Many émigré scientists had fled the persecution of the Nazi regime. Anxiety and fear for their relatives in Europe haunted them constantly and drove them to work feverishly to end the war. The air was thick with accents of many countries. One security guard was overheard to remark that he wasn't bothered by security half as much as by trying to understand all the foreign languages.

And as ugly and ramshackle as Los Alamos was, it was surrounded by some of the most spectacular scenery in America. Residents of the Hill had an unsurpassed view across the mountains and desert.

"Behind us lay the Sangre de Cristo Mountains, at sunset bathed in changing waves of color—scarlets and lavenders," wrote Ruth Marshak, Project wife and third grade teacher, describing her arrival on the mesa top. "Below was the desert with its flatness, broken by majestic palisades, that seemed like the ruined cathedrals and palaces of some old, great vanished race. Ahead was Los Alamos, and beyond the flat plateau on which it sat was its backdrop, the Jemez Mountain Range. Whenever things went wrong at Los Alamos, and there was never a day when they didn't, we had this one consolation—we had a view."[14]

Regular Sunday outings to nearby Bandelier National Monument took the community off the mesa. The women would set out the picnic lunches and care for the babies, leaving the older children free to explore the canyon and the ruins. The fathers would walk apart, oblivious to the beauty of their surroundings, deep in thought and discussion

Los Alamos Historical Society

Dorothy often attended Los Alamos parties, here with I.I. Rabi, Robert Oppenheimer and Victor Weisskopf at the Oppenheimer home in Los Alamos about 1944.

of their work. In addition to hiking, horseback riding, ice skating, and downhill skiing were all favorite sports.

Saturday night parties were another integral part of mesa life. "The biggest and brassiest parties were undoubtedly the dorm parties, so called," wrote Bernice Brode, " because one entire dormitory of young men gave the party....There were always too many people, too much noise, and too much liquor, but we always had a wonderful time and looked forward to the next one before we had recovered from the last."[15]

In December 1943 another slice of life was added to the mix at Los Alamos. The British Mission, a group of distinguished scientists associated with Britain's atomic weapons project, began arriving on the Hill to work in "full and effective collaboration" with the American scientists. President Roosevelt and Prime Minister Winston Churchill personally worked out this arrangement after months of negotiating and hard bargaining over the degree of access British scientists would have to U.S. atomic research centers. The forty-person mission was led by James Chadwick, a Nobel laureate who, like Oppenheimer, had worked at the Cavendish Laboratory in Cambridge, England.

One of the first to arrive was Otto Frisch, who had been working at Liverpool University with Chadwick when he was asked to join the Los Alamos contingent. In addition to his talents as a scientist, Frisch was a fine piano player and cartoonist who enjoyed a lively social life on the Hill. Niels Bohr and his physicist son, Aage, were other early arrivals. Bohr began to serve as consultant to the British atomic weapons group after his escape from Nazi-occupied Denmark in the fall of 1943. His presence at Los Alamos was enormous, both as a scientist and a humanist. Another member of the mission was Klaus Fuchs, a German-born physicist who had fled to Britain. After the war, he was imprisoned for disclosing atomic secrets to the Russians. Fuchs, an excellent dancer, was popular on the Hill and a much sought-after babysitter because children liked him and parents trusted him.

The arrival of the British Mission was a high point for Dorothy McKibbin, too. She loved having "Uncle Nick" come to 109 East Palace and enjoyed helping the British wives acclimate to a most un-British way of living. Daily life in Los Alamos enhanced an accepted British stereotype of frontier America: new self-contained towns, isolated by rugged terrain, and surrounded by Indians.

The British scientists stayed for two years. At the end of the war, the British Mission gave a formal farewell party for their friends on the Hill. Residents of the mesa dressed sedately in full evening regalia. A few women even managed to find long white gloves; some men wore white tie and tails, and a faint odor of mothballs. Steak and kidney pie was the main course with trifle for dessert. After dinner, the Brits performed an original skit titled "Babes in the Woods." The entertainment was a smash hit, and the party a great finale to the "Grand Alliance." Dorothy noted that the climax was reached when "everyone rose to their feet, brandishing a paper cup, and drank the King's health with sparkling burgundy."[16]

Los Alamos Historical Society

Edith Warner at home by the Rio Grande

Dinner at the home of Dorothy's friend, Edith Warner, was a special treat for a small number of Hill families. In the summer of 1937, Robert Oppenheimer had ridden on horseback into the area and stopped at her tea room for refreshment. He stayed all afternoon and fell under the spell of the little house and the woman who tended it. In 1943, Oppenheimer was able to persuade the military authorities to let small groups of men and women go down from the Hill for dinner at the house by the Rio Grande. One or two groups came nearly every night. Seating was often booked for weeks in advance. Miss Warner preferred to have no more than ten at a time, but she would add a reservation for special dignitaries such as Niels Bohr and his son. Dinner cost $2 per person.

Guests ate by candlelight with the only other illumination coming from the corner fireplaces, which Tilano laid with piñon logs. He and Edith served the home-cooked food on black pottery plates and bowls made by Maria Martinez, the famed potter of San Ildefonso. Dressed in a shirtwaist dress with her gray hair wrapped in a coil at the nape of her neck, Edith frowned on loud talk and maintained an atmosphere of quiet dignity.

Dorothy was a frequent dinner guest and fondly recalls the food there. "I remember her ragout of lamb, and fresh fruit and vegetables, lush raspberries in summer, and her chocolate cake. That cake was famous around the country; it was delicious! There was no secret about its recipe, and many people tried to make it but it never tasted as good as Edith's."[17]

In addition to brief interludes in Santa Fe, dinners at Edith Warner's, Sunday picnics and outings, and Saturday night parties, there were many other diversions on the Hill. A town council was created in August 1943. Members were elected by popular vote for six-month terms. The council was responsible for discussing problems affecting community welfare and reporting its findings and recommendations to Groves and Oppenheimer. Housing-assignment policy, traffic control, and the licensing and management of dogs were among the matters on the council agenda. The council's most important task was "maintaining a spirit of community cooperation directed toward a single objective, the efficiency and success of the Project."[18]

More than thirty recreational and cultural organizations were formed during the early years. Hollywood movies were shown several times a week; an array of local talent provided theatricals. Music and dance were important entertainments. Folks walking along the roads in the evening enjoyed strains of Bach or Beethoven or Mozart filling the air. Chamber music groups sprang up; small informal gatherings met in almost every neighborhood for practice. A mesa-top radio station played a wide array of music, garnered from the extensive record collections of Hill residents. There were two organized singing groups, a small group of twelve auditioned singers and the Mesa Chorus, open to anyone who wanted to sing. The chorus performed Handel's *Messiah* each year. Square dancing was the rage, and couples danced schottisches, polkas, and waltzes to music provided by the pooled record collections. A chronic shortage of female partners meant that men could take an occasional break while women danced continuously.

Los Alamos was a mud patch with a trailblazing spirit. "We felt like the first ones that came with the Mayflower," recalled Austrian physicist Victor Weisskopf.[19] There was an aura of constant excitement in the whole experience, and wonderful parties, entertainments, and discussions, all conducted with extraordinary people in an atmosphere of intense urgency.

Chapter 13

TRINITY AND THE END OF THE WAR

Development of the uranium bomb, a gun-type bomb, moved ahead confidently. Work on the implosion plutonium weapon was slow and frustrating with many unknowns. Since the implosion method was so far removed from any existing practices, it became apparent that in order to plan for the future, it would have to be tested.

In the spring of 1944, scientists began preparations to test the plutonium bomb. Kenneth Bainbridge, a Harvard physics professor with a background in electrical engineering, was put in charge of the test. The Alamogordo bombing range in the desolate Jornada del Muerto (Journey of the Dead) area, one hundred twenty miles south of Albuquerque, two hundred miles from Los Alamos, was chosen as the test site.

The air base at Alamogordo, where B-29 crews received their final training before leaving for the Pacific, had the advantage of already being under government control. Few ranchers were living in the area, but they were unwilling to move out because they had no idea why they were being asked to leave their homes. Eventually the Army persuaded them to vacate their property. Oppenheimer selected "Trinity" as the code name for the test that was scheduled to take place in July 1945. Just what "Trinity" meant to Robert has long been a subject of conjecture and is generally attributed to the fourteenth of John Donne's Holy Sonnets, which opens "Batter my heart, three-person'd God."[1]

At Los Alamos preparation for the first test of an atomic weapon was proceeding at a fever pitch when, on April 12, 1945, residents of the Hill were stunned by the sudden death of President Roosevelt. He had served his nation as president for twelve years, and many simply could not imagine a world without his leadership. Bernice Brode described the response at Los Alamos when news of Roosevelt's death reached them:

> We were all aware that Los Alamos was a special project of the President and we were all personally affected. When the news came over the loud speaker in the Tech Area, crowds gathered and everyone wondered what would become of the project now, since Truman, who would succeed to the presidency, did not know of our existence. A pall settled over our town. There was a memorial service in the theater, at which Oppenheimer spoke, and everyone was quiet and thoughtful, emotionally moved at the loss of a great man. V-E day, which came a month later [May 8, 1945], did not have the impact on our Mesa that the death of Roosevelt did.[2]

Within twenty-four hours of Roosevelt's death, President Harry Truman was told about the atomic bomb. After the unconditional surrender of Germany, he proposed a summit meeting with the Russians and the British to discuss the future of a postwar world. Based on available data about the progress of preparations at Alamogordo, the meeting was scheduled for July 15 at Potsdam, near Berlin. Truman had come to believe that, in a large measure, his success in resolving major international issues would depend on the results of that test.

At 109 East Palace, Dorothy felt the tension building on the Hill. She said that she just felt it in her bones. Seventy people, on average, checked into her office every day for transport to the mesa. Telephone calls were too numerous to count; voices were strained and anxious. With a sudden influx of visiting dignitaries, she sensed that things were reaching a climax. On one occasion, she had to house a general and a sergeant in one bed at La Fonda. To quiet the fuss, the explanation was, as usual, "There's a war on, you know!"

On Sunday, July 15, two young couples from the Hill invited Dorothy to join them for an evening picnic on Sandia Peak in Albuquerque. When she told Kevin of this invitation, he began to gather his gear and prepare to join her. It was one of the few times he remembers being excluded from her outings. She did not give him a reason. She knew something about the forthcoming test and surmised she was not going on an ordinary picnic. By nightfall, the skies had darkened. Thunder rolled in the surrounding mountains, and it began to rain. The rain continued through the night. The test, scheduled for 4:00 a.m., was delayed for one hour and then another thirty minutes.

Precisely at 5:30 a.m., July 16, 1945, the first atomic device exploded. The explosion came as an intense light flash, a sudden wave of heat, and later, a tremendous roar as the shock wave passed and echoed in the valley. A ball of fire rose rapidly, followed by a multicolored mushroom cloud extending to 40,000 feet. The light from the explosion extended even to Sandia Peak where Dorothy and her friends were watching. "The feeling of awe I had when that light hit us was remarkable," Dorothy said. "The leaves of those native green trees were shining with a gold. It was different. The world had changed. It would never be the same again. Nothing would ever be the same again."[3]

Groves, who had planned to hold a series of meetings at Alamogordo after the blast, changed his mind:

> The plans proved utterly impractical, for no one who had witnessed the test was in a frame of mind to discuss anything. The reaction to success was too great. It was not only that we had achieved success with the bomb; but that everyone—scientists, military officers and engineers—realized that we

> had been personal participants in, and eyewitnesses to, a major milestone in the world's history and had a sobering appreciation of what the results of our work would be.[4]

There was no celebration at the test site or on the Hill. The men had done the job the government had asked them to do. They were relieved that it had been successful. They were not elated. It had been too terrible a sight for that emotion. "They had seen what no one had seen before," Dorothy wrote, "and it was so awesome in its terrible beauty and its blazing horror that none who saw it would ever know innocence again. The brief moment was burned on their minds and into the innermost shadows of their spirits."[5]

News of the successful test reached President Truman at Potsdam on July 21. It made a profound impact on him and Prime Minister Churchill. The atomic bomb had the potential of eliminating the need for an invasion of Japan and, at the same time, would provide the Japanese with an honorable reason to surrender. Possibly, the war could now end quickly. Truman also knew that he no longer needed Russian help to finish the war in the Far East. On July 24 he told Premier Joseph Stalin about the bomb. Truman commented that Stalin's reply was unexpectedly cool and brief. By that time Klaus Fuchs and other spies had provided the Russians with a detailed picture of the recently tested weapon. For nearly two years, the Soviets had been working on a fission weapon of their own. On July 26 the U.S., British, and Chinese governments issued an ultimatum to the Japanese government, confronting Japan with a choice between unconditional surrender and total annihilation.

Scientists at Los Alamos and laboratories across the country were beginning to discuss postwar plans for the use of atomic energy. In late July Dorothy's house was the site of a one-day meeting, attended by Enrico Fermi, Samuel Allison, an experimental physicist and protégé of Arthur Compton at the University of Chicago, and a number of other scientists from Los Alamos and the Met Lab. The result of their day's work was the organization of the Institute of Nuclear Research at the University of Chicago. Later it became the Enrico Fermi Institute; Allison served as its first director. On August 9, 1945, a press release announced the formation of the Institute.

During this period Dorothy issued her one and only pass without prior authorization.

A young man arrived during the noon hour and the offices on the Hill were shut down," she recalled. "He was in a hurry. He looked honest and sounded as if he knew where he was going and who he was supposed to see. So I looked him over carefully, shot my whole future to the winds, maybe, with an unprecedented and wild action. With calm and firm letters, I wrote out a pass to Col. Paul Tibbets, the pilot of the Enola Gay, who would drop the bomb on Hiroshima."[6]

Right after the test at Alamogordo, a large crew of scientists left Los Alamos for the Pacific island of Tinian to make the final adjustments to the uranium, gun-type bomb dubbed "Little Boy." The plutonium implosion bomb was called "Fat Man."

Three weeks after the Trinity test, on August 6, "Little Boy" destroyed Hiroshima, which had escaped extensive damage during the war, making it a logical target for the first atomic bomb. The previous evening, a colleague had called Dorothy to suggest that she bring a radio to work in the morning. Dorothy placed the small radio on her desk and turned it on low. About eleven o'clock that morning, a voice came through and said, "This is Harry Truman speaking, and I want to tell you that the bomb that was dropped on Hiroshima was made in the mountains of New Mexico."

At lunch that day Dorothy told Kevin, "That was our bomb." There was a long silence between them as Dorothy, conditioned for more than two years not to even whisper the name "Los Alamos" or say the word "physicist," realized what she had done. Then she paused; her arm shot across the table and caught his wrist. She said in a tense, alarmed voice, "But don't you tell anybody."[7] The next day, the *New Mexican*, the Santa Fe newspaper, ran full front-page coverage of the story. Mrs. Field, the owner of 109 East Palace, came running in to Dorothy's office and said excitedly, "So that is what you have been doing!"

On August 9, Nagasaki was demolished by Fat Man. Five days later, Japan gave up the fight. Surrender ceremonies were held on September 2. Thirty years later, Dorothy summed up her thoughts about Hiroshima, Nagasaki, and the end of World War II:

> "Who sows the wind will reap the whirlwind" was discovered long years before, in another time and another place. In the summer of 1945, it was they, the scientists of the Manhattan Project, who had sown the wind. The whirlwind they had reaped was an enormity greater than they had imagined it could be. And within the next few weeks twice again they had faced knowledge of the unbearable horror they had fashioned. In those twice again moments, the horror was unleashed not on a desert place but on men and women and children.
>
> The war was ended. No more fire bombings. No more beaches littered vilely with hundreds and thousands of young men who should be on the playing fields or peering through a microscope in a college classroom at bits and pieces of the universe, or dreaming of spinning a sextant and flying to the stars. The war was over. No more man killing man. But the sin did not go away. The physicists—those who had imagined what could happen if this and this were possible, and those who took these images and made them fact—these physicists determined that there should be an end to playing withcosmic fire. Literally, almost to a man, they determined not to make the Super [the hydrogen bomb].[8]

In answer to the question, "Was the development of the atomic bomb necessary?" General Groves replied unequivocally, "Yes." To the question, "Is atomic energy a force for good or for evil?" he could only say, "As mankind wills it."[9]

At the end of the war, the scientists took immediate steps to create educational groups to explain the nature of atomic power to the people. "Because of 'weird and dangerous conclusions' being circulated in print and on the radio," Dorothy wrote, "they believed it was necessary to present facts before panic destroyed the meaning of science."[10]

By the autumn of 1945, local groups were formed for this purpose at Los Alamos and other leading laboratories. There was no intent or even an idea at the time of becoming political. They placed their spokesmen on local radio stations and their papers in local libraries. Members also contributed articles to newspapers and periodicals. Meanwhile, rumors from Washington had reached the Hill that a bill for the continued military control of all atomic energy was being pushed through Congress without debate. Clearly, this legislation was a threat to their futures. More than any other group in the country, the Los Alamos atomic scientists were in the unique position of understanding this new energy and knowing how it could be used. The Congressmen and the public were in the dark.

On the evening of August 30, 1945, determined to act as a group and influence postwar atomic policy, nearly five hundred members of the Los Alamos scientific community met in Theater Two (the largest meeting place in Los Alamos) to create the Association of Los Alamos Scientists (ALAS). They formed a committee to draft a statement on the postwar importance of atomic energy. They were "united in their concern about the implication of the nuclear monster they had helped create."[11] Similar organizations were formed at other government war projects; jointly they became the national Federation of Atomic Scientists.

Part Four
AFTER THE BOMB

Chapter 14

THE FUTURE OF LOS ALAMOS

At the end of World War II there was no clear agreement on the future of the Los Alamos Scientific Laboratory. Most scientists were eager to leave the Hill. The Nobel laureates were the first to go. Many of the young physicists who had been on leave resumed their interrupted academic careers. Oppenheimer, who had an array of offers, announced his intention to resign in October 1945. Like so many of his colleagues, he wanted to go back to teaching and expected to return to California.

On October 16 Brig. Gen. Leslie Groves came from Washington to present a Certificate of Appreciation to the laboratory from the Secretary of War. Dorothy saw Oppenheimer just before the ceremony, spoke to him briefly, and noted that "his eyes were glazed over, the way they were when he was in deep thought. Afterwards, I realized that in those few moments, Robert had been preparing his acceptance speech."[1] She found the speech touching and one of his best.

The front of Fuller Lodge was decked in flags. Groves made a speech acknowledging the important work done by the laboratory. Then Oppenheimer, on his last day as director, speaking in a low, quiet voice, struck a theme that would fill the next decade of his life:

Los Alamos Historical Society

Oppenheimer, far left, spoke quietly to accept the Certificate of Appreciation.

> It is our hope that in years to come we may look at this scroll, and all that it signifies, with pride.
>
> Today that pride must be tempered with a profound concern. If atomic bombs are to be added as new weapons to the arsenals of a warring world, or to the arsenals of nations preparing for war, then the time will come when mankind will curse the names of Los Alamos and Hiroshima.
>
> The peoples of the world must unite, or they will perish. This war, that has ravaged so much of the earth, has written these words. The atomic bomb has spelled them out for all men to understand. Other men have spoken them, in other times, of other wars, of other weapons. They have not prevailed. There are some, misled by a false sense of human history, who hold that they will not prevail today. It is not for us to believe that. By our works we are committed, committed to a world united, before the common peril, in law, and in humanity.[2]

Despite her relief that the war was over and that the Los Alamos scientists had achieved their goal in twenty-seven remarkable months, Dorothy's heart was heavy over the departure of Robert Oppenheimer, whom she adored and whose friendship brought her such great pleasure. There was also uncertainty about the future of her job. Her important role as the gatekeeper and "mother superior" was certain to change or possibly be eliminated.

Norris Bradbury, the Berkeley-trained Navy physicist who had organized the assembly of the Trinity bomb, was Oppenheimer's choice to succeed him as laboratory director. Bradbury, who had planned to return to a teaching position at Stanford, accepted the position for six months; he was at the helm for the next twenty-five years.

In the early months of his tenure, the Los Alamos lab was in a struggle for its existence. Decision-makers in Washington were slow to acknowledge the need to support the lab for future atomic weapons research and development. Once they realized its importance, Bradbury made a commitment to build suitable permanent housing for the laboratory staff and rebuild a scientific team to work on future bomb design. The Santa Fe office was retained, and Dorothy continued as the "chargé d'affaires."

Many of the strictures of life on the Hill that had been mere annoyances during the war became intolerable in a peacetime community. Bradbury quickly ended censorship of all mail and recommended that friends and relatives be allowed to visit the mesa.

Throughout the early years of the Manhattan Project, there was great curiosity in Santa Fe about the influx of hundreds of new people who came into the area and claimed only one address, P.O. Box 1663, Santa Fe, a city in which none of them ever lived. In December 1945 the Army's secrecy ban was lifted, and residents of the Hill made a grand debut into the society of Santa Fe. It was staged by a special committee of Santa Fe citizens at the Museum of Anthropology, located across the road from Dorothy McKibbin's house. The museum replaced its Indian exhibits with pictures of atomic experiments and Hiroshima damage. The main event was a program of speeches, followed by a question and answer period and an elegant reception.

"The audience was most interested to see the 'secret' people and to hear their opinions about the hope and dangers of the new atomic age," Bernice Brode wrote. "Not one of us expressed a sense of guilt—

Los Alamos Historical Society

Post-war exhibits intrigued Santa Fe residents long curious about what was going on up on the Hill.

quite the contrary, but many emphasized the dangers of uncontrolled use of such bombs for the future."[3]

That occasion opened up a new social world for Los Alamos residents who had lived in secrecy and isolation for over two years. They were invited to many parties, all coordinated by Dorothy with her wide network of Santa Fe friends. Hostesses sent word to her about the type of party and the number of scientists and wives to be invited. Dorothy forwarded these invitations to the Hill where they were posted on a bulletin board, and those interested would sign up to attend. The wives were thrilled with this turn of events and were delighted to be in real homes. They loved meeting the leaders of Santa Fe society: writers, artists, architects, stimulating people of varied backgrounds and ages, who were an enchanting antidote to the drabness of Los Alamos and the sameness of its homogeneous population. Yet it was the men that the Santa Fe residents were so eager to meet. After one or two parties and driving eighty miles round trip in cold winter weather at night, the scientists balked. They were not accustomed to being in the limelight and were embarrassed by so much attention. But for the women it was fun while it lasted.

The formation of a Santa Fe Citizens' Committee for Atomic Energy was another outgrowth of the Santa Fe museum meeting. The poet Witter Bynner, one of Dorothy's dearest friends, was the president of that group. He wrote a barrage of poems, printed in the *New Mexican,* extolling the new atomic age and its scientists. The Santa Fe committee raised money for the Association of Los Alamos Scientists, giving the organization some "cash on hand" for the first time.

In December the women on the Hill invited their new friends to come up to Los Alamos for a tour. The Santa Feans dropped all previous engagements and eagerly accepted the opportunity to enter the mystery town. Preparations for this reciprocal visit turned out to be more complicated than first envisioned. It took great persuasive talents to get Army security to go along with such a plan after years of carefully guarded isolation. When permission was finally granted, Dorothy was in charge of creating the invitation list and calling the Santa Fe guests from her office. She instructed all prospective visitors about the pass system to Los Alamos and made certain that she had the exact information about each guest who would go through the security gate. Dorothy worried that most of the Santa Fe guests would not understand the need for the passes. As residents of a small town, they were accustomed to going about their business freely and were usually recognized by local shopkeepers and officeholders. In addition, many did not drive and planned to have chauffeurs bring them to the mesa. The Army had not counted on an entourage of civilian chauffeurs and was ready to call off the whole deal. Once again, Dorothy came to the rescue and organized military car pools to transport Santa Fe guests to the Hill.

On the day of the scheduled event, the water shortage from the summer drought reached an acute stage. No toilets flushed; the taps were dry. The water line froze. Even though most of the food was prepared and everything else was in order, it seemed impossible to give a party without running water. The planners decided to call it off. They telephoned Dorothy who relayed the change in plans to the disappointed guests. Then Norris Bradbury arranged with the Army to shuttle trucks of water from the river ten miles below up to the old water tower where the ladies of Los Alamos could fill pots and pans to cook the meal. Sensing that a party was just what they needed to take their minds off the demoralizing water crisis, they decided to go ahead with the party after all. Once again the good-sport Dorothy was recruited to call all the guests and declare the party on. Bernice Brode wrote, "Dorothy was wonderful and never once accused us of being erratic, to say the least."[4]

The day was cold and cloudy. Festivities began mid-afternoon. Guests were expected to arrive at 3:00 p.m., but some were an hour early. So tea at Fuller Lodge was served before the tour, and the juggling began. Plans for the dinner party, which was to be a movable feast, at which the guests would move from house to house for each course, changed when the guests settled into the first house they visited and wanted to stay there. So the food was moved from house to house.

Apparently, the guests were so appalled by the living conditions at Los Alamos that they were in a state of shock. One Santa Fe lady was heard to say, "I can't get over it, such nice people living in such a place all this time." Dorothy telephoned the Hill a few days later to report that the city of Santa Fe was now divided into two parts: "those who had seen and those who had not seen."

Chapter 15

KEVIN LEAVES HOME

In March of 1946, the University of California renewed its contract to operate the Los Alamos Scientific Laboratory; the following January the Manhattan Project was transferred from the management of the Army to the Atomic Energy Commission. For another eighteen years, Dorothy continued to be the official welcoming committee for newcomers who came to work at the lab.

Eventually the intensity of the pace slowed. Dorothy concentrated her peacetime efforts on screening applicants and managing a hostess program to provide information about schools, churches, clubs, and medical care to incoming wives. To boost housewife morale on the Hill, she established a shopping service, tracking down wanted goods not available at the Army PX. She provided house-hunting assistance for the hundreds of new employees acquired during the laboratory's long-term recruiting campaign in the late 1940s and 1950s when the Los Alamos population exceeded 10,000.

In those years Dorothy and Kevin continued to enjoy the fiestas and dances at the Indian pueblos. He attended the local schools through junior high and had a brief stint at Phillips Andover Academy, a boarding school for boys in Andover, Massachusetts. This young man who loved to "potter about" the Santa Fe area, collecting snakes and horny toads, making his own entertainment and enjoying his own company, was a "good enough" student in an uncompetitive public school system. However, there was nothing in his background that would have prepared him academically or socially for the rigors of one of the most prestigious college preparatory schools in the country.

Kevin notes that "my mother got me into Phillips Andover with a lot of help from old friends of my father in St. Paul and his Princeton classmates," men who had contributed to a trust fund for Kevin's education at the time of Joe's death.[1] Dorothy was honoring what she thought Joe would have wanted for his son and what her parents expected for their grandson. Given Dorothy's educational background, the Scarritt family tradition of sending sons east to college, and Joe McKibbin's experience at a Pennsylvania boarding school before Princeton, she was determined to give Kevin the same opportunity

In the fall of 1946, Dorothy and Kevin loaded up her 1941 Chevrolet convertible and drove to Andover by way of New York City. About a week before they left on their trip, a friend of Dorothy's called and asked Kevin to come out to her house to get a rattlesnake out of her chicken coop. He complied, put the three-foot prairie rattlesnake in a large jar, and took it home. For some unknown reason, the rattlesnake went with them on their eastern journey.

Kevin recalls, "We were staying at a hotel which I think was on Fifth Avenue. We took the car to a parking garage and left it there for three or four days. We went to Broadway shows and saw the original cast of *Oklahoma*. We went to the Brooklyn Zoo, Central Park, and, of course, rode the subway. Gee, we had a wonderful time."[2]

The parking garage was close to the hotel. When it was time to head north to Massachusetts, they went over to the garage. Kevin gave the claim ticket to the attendant. He and his mother started walking back to where they could see the car on the first floor. They were heading toward it, and all of a sudden one man and then another came running out, shouting at them and said, "Hey, you can't go back there!" Then Kevin noticed there was a big sign on the car, warning of the presence of a rattlesnake. It was immediately apparent to Kevin and Dorothy that someone had been poking around in the car and found the snake, sitting placidly in its jar, behind the back seat of the convertible. The men had to be snooping around in the car, because it was impossible to see into that area when the top was up. Kevin explained to the garage attendants that he and his mother knew the rattlesnake was in there. Finally the car was released to them, and they took off for Andover.

As parents did in those days, Dorothy stayed around Andover for a week. With her talent for problem-solving and discovering just the right solution in unusual circumstances, she found a local animal farm that was willing to house the snake. In fact, the zoo director was delighted with this addition and made a plaque for its cage which read, "Prairie Rattlesnake, Gift of Kevin McKibbin, Santa Fe, New Mexico."

For Kevin, Andover was a whole new world:

> The environment and the culture were like another planet. You talk about culture shock! At home in school I wore an old pair of levis and a shirt. At Andover I had a pair of gray flannel slacks, a sport coat and a tie. It was a change that I would not or could not adapt to. You had to close yourself up in your room at night and not associate with anyone and study. I did not know how to study, and I was not a very good student. I met some nice classmates who were in my dormitory. I left Andover at Christmas time to go home, and when I got home I told my mother I was not going back. I know I shot her right in the heart when I told her that. She just didn't flinch, wanted to know why I didn't want to give it a go. I just said it was not my world, and I didn't want to return. This was probably one of my mother's biggest disappointments, but she never dwelt on it.[3]

Dorothy's response to Kevin's decision was typical of her approach to life. She took things as they came to her and moved forward.

In the summer of 1947, on a visit to Santa Fe, Dorothy's 84-

year-old mother fell and broke her hip. She died in Dorothy's house the following November. Friends note that Dorothy was "more relieved than bereaved" by her mother's death. Two years later, on February 27, 1949, Arthur Davis Scarritt, Dorothy's brother, died of cancer after an eight-month illness. Now Dorothy and her brother, Bill, eleven years her senior, were the only surviving members of her Kansas City family.

Kevin graduated from Santa Fe High School in the spring of 1949. That fall he entered New Mexico A&M, now New Mexico State University in Las Cruces. At the end of his freshman year, he got a summer job at the Los Alamos Scientific Laboratory. On weekends he raced an old 1935 Ford coupe on a little track in Santa Fe. During that summer, only five years after the end of World War II, the North Koreans invaded South Korea. Kevin and his fellow workers, most of them of draft age, followed the fighting intensely.

In the fall of 1950, Kevin transferred to the University of Colorado. When he came home at Christmas, he got together with his high school friends, most of whom were planning to join the Korean war effort. Fearful of being drafted and put into the fiercest fighting of the war, they decided to enlist in the Army. At that time recruitment for the Air Force, Navy, and Coast Guard were "frozen" with more men volunteering than were needed, and none felt "tough enough" to join the Marines.

Kevin and his friends went by bus to Albuquerque. There they boarded a troop train that took them to Fort Sill in Lawton, Oklahoma, where Kevin's father had served in World War I. They were processed there and sent to Fort Bragg in Fayetteville, North Carolina, for twelve weeks of extensive training under the direction of men who had served at the Korean front. At the end of this training period, Dorothy drove Kevin's car to North Carolina. He was delighted to have his own wheels again for his next assignment, a leadership course at Fort Jackson, South Carolina, followed by Officer Training School at Fort Knox, Kentucky.

On New Year's Eve 1951, Kevin was passing through Kansas City on Christmas leave. He asked his aunt, Anna Scarritt, A.D.'s widow, to arrange dates for him and two of his friends. Anna loved the role of matchmaker and came up with three women. From years of visiting Kansas City at the Christmas holiday season and later in the summer, Kevin knew them all and chose Mary Gower Thompson, who broke another date to spend the evening with him. That was the beginning of a lifelong relationship. Mary Gower, known as "M.G.," was then a senior at Vassar College in Poughkeepsie, New York, her mother's alma mater. M.G. had attended the Sunset Hill School, a private college preparatory high school for girls in Kansas City, co-founded by her maternal grandmother. She and Kevin corresponded regularly over the next year.

In the winter of 1952, when Kevin was assigned to duty in Korea, he flew out of the United States from Travis Air Force Base near San Francisco. Dorothy went out to be with him, and they spent a weekend in the wine country of Napa Valley. The next day Kevin flew to Japan and from there went on a troop ship to Inchon Harbor in Korea. Because of his college background and Army training, he was put into a counterfire platoon of about twenty men who worked with electronic instrumentation on the front line.

In March 1953, Kevin got his orders to "rotate" assignments to the United States. When Dorothy heard that Kevin was coming home, she was ecstatic! Of course, she wanted to meet his ship, but all Kevin knew was that it would be coming into harbor somewhere on the West Coast. Dorothy, in her usual resourceful manner, contacted an old Los Alamos friend who was high up in the Navy. He found the exact location of Kevin's arrival. It was a thrilling moment for Kevin when his ship landed in Seattle, and there was Dorothy waving to him from the dock! They returned to Santa Fe the next day. Kevin had a thirty-day leave before he was to report to Fort Sill.

Official photograph U.S.Navy

Dorothy was on hand in Seattle to welcome Kevin home from overseas.

Old friends note that the year Kevin served overseas in the Korean conflict was the one time in Dorothy's life when her optimism failed her. She missed him terribly and feared she would lose him in battle. In addition, her eyesight had begun to fail. In the summer of 1952, when she was 55 years old, she had her first cataract operation. In those days, following cataract surgery, a patient had to lie flat in bed for ten days with little movement. She scheduled the second operation for one year later. Both enhanced her ability to see although she was forced to wear thick glasses.

When Kevin returned to Santa Fe, he invited Mary Gower to visit him there. She and her father came by train to the station in Lamy, sixteen miles south of Santa Fe. Dorothy and Kevin met them and took them to a restaurant on Canyon Road featuring spicy New Mexican food. Years later, M.G. recalled this inauspicious meal. "It nearly killed my father. He took one bite, and I took about half a bite. Meanwhile Kevin and his mother ate everything and said, 'Oh, this is so good.'"[4]

M.G. and her father stayed about a week during which there was another memorable meal. At dinner time one evening, Mary Gower got a telephone call from another suitor, a sports announcer in Kansas City. Kevin answered the telephone, and M.G. took the call just around the corner from where the families were gathered. "So we were listening and got the drift that there was something heady going on here," said Kevin. "After a while, she came out and said, 'That takes care of that!'" Her father looked visibly relieved, since neither he nor Mrs. Thompson approved of the sports announcer."[5] Kevin quickly asked M.G. to marry him. They set the wedding date for January 1954, when his military service would end.

Kevin went to Fort Sill where he had an eight-to-five job. On the weekends he commuted to Kansas City to visit Mary Gower. After a short while, they decided to get married on June 30, 1953, her parents' twenty-fifth wedding anniversary. While Dorothy was in her element getting lists together and relishing a major social event in Kansas City, Mary Gower's mother was less enthusiastic about the date and thought Kevin and M.G. were stealing the limelight from her anniversary celebration. Others wondered if the change in plans meant that M.G. was pregnant. Their first child was born six years later.

Laura Gilpin, 1954

Kevin and Mary Gower Thompson were married in 1953.

Although the wedding ceremony was small, more than two hundred people attended the reception at the country club. It was a grand affair. The occasion was a source of great satisfaction to Dorothy, uniting two highly respected families of Kansas City in a style that would have pleased Joe McKibbin. Although Dorothy was a spirited risk-taker throughout her life, she was also guided by a strong sense of propriety and gentility. She wanted to do the "right thing" and was pleased that Kevin had "married well."

Chapter 16

DOROTHY AND THE OPPENHEIMER ORDEAL

With Kevin's safe return from Korea and the pleasure of his marriage, Dorothy had much to celebrate in the summer of 1953. However, her joy in these events gave way to anguish and heartbreak with Robert Oppenheimer's extraordinary ordeal that ultimately led to the loss of his security clearance in June 1954.

From 1941 to 1955, with minor exceptions, Oppenheimer was subjected to constant scrutiny by agents of his own government. He was followed, his phone was tapped, his mail was opened, and his offices and homes were bugged. He once commented that the U.S. government spent more money on his surveillance than it paid him in salary as the Los Alamos laboratory director.[1]

Given this intense observation, it is fascinating to think of the many quiet evenings Robert spent at Dorothy's house, an oasis from the unsightly settlement of Los Alamos and a respite from the urgency and relentless stress of building the bomb. What a comfort Dorothy must have been to him and how she delighted in his friendship.

When Oppenheimer left Los Alamos to return to California in the fall of 1945, he intended to devote himself full time to the teaching of physics. Although he worked hard to immerse himself in academic duties at Berkeley and Caltech, he was repeatedly summoned to Washington to develop a plan for the international control of atomic energy. Between 1946 and 1953, he served as scientist-adviser to more than a dozen governmental committees concerned with the control and application of atomic energy. In January 1947 he began a six-year term as member of the General Advisory Committee (GAC) to the U.S. Atomic Energy Commission (AEC). He was elected chairman of the GAC on the first day the committee met.

The following October Oppenheimer assumed the directorship of the Institute for Advanced Study in Princeton. The primary purpose of the Institute was, and still is, "the pursuit of advanced learning and exploration in fields of pure science and high scholarship."[2] Professors carry on their scholarly work without having to offer formal courses. Emphasis is on the informal interaction of scholars in a community of intellectuals, a natural place for Oppenheimer with his brilliant mind and insatiable quest for knowledge.

Nineteen forty-eight was a year of rising fame and influence for Robert Oppenheimer. He had become known widely as the "father of the A-Bomb," was president of the American Physical Society , and in that year achieved the "accolade of pure fame"[3]—his portrait on the front cover of *Time* magazine. His prominence within the scientific community was acknowledged in the cover chosen for the inaugural issue of *Physics Today.* The picture showed a pork pie hat sitting on a piece of industrial equipment.

Although Robert had risen to celebrity status as an adviser within some government circles, he continued to live under the unrelenting attention of federal investigators. When the House Un-American Activities Committee (HUAC) began investigating alleged Communist penetration of the Berkeley Radiation Laboratory during the early days of World War II, a net began to spread over Oppenheimer. On June 7,

1949, he appeared before a session of HUAC. Members of the press were not allowed in the room. He was questioned about the Communist activities of several of his former students, his brother Frank, and his close friend Haakon Chevalier, an instructor in French literature at Berkeley. In 1943, after Robert had been named director of the Los Alamos laboratory, he and Chevalier had a conversation in which Chevalier told him about a scientist who claimed he could transmit secret technical information to the Soviets. Oppenheimer emphatically told Chevalier he would have no part of such an activity. However, eight months passed before Robert reported the conversation to security officials.

Dorothy was present at that HUAC hearing. She had gone to Washington after her thirtieth class reunion at Smith to visit Luvie and Drew Pearson. Luvie was an old friend from Santa Fe. Her husband was a newspaperman who wrote "The Washington Merry Go Round," a political column syndicated in newspapers across the country. Upon her arrival, Dorothy learned that Oppenheimer was being questioned that very morning. At once she took a cab to Capitol Hill and entered the crowded hearing room.

"On a chair facing the six inquisitors [members of HUAC] ensconced on their dais sat Robert, sprayed by strong lights, a lone figure," she wrote. "I slipped into a seat midway in the hall and purely by chance found myself beside Anne Wilson Marks [the former secretary to Oppenheimer after Priscilla Duffield left Los Alamos]. I whispered to her, 'How can he see his notes with lights in his eyes?' Anne's answer was, 'He has no notes.' I was shocked. I did not wait to speak to him that day, but slipped out at lunch break as unobtrusively as I had entered."[4]

Despite the lack of notes, Oppenheimer's power of persuasion charmed the Congressmen who came forward after his testimony to shake his hand. Only six days later, on June 13, Oppenheimer, in his role as chairman of the AEC's General Advisory Committee, testified before the Joint Committee on Atomic Energy, which was investigating a charge that the infant Atomic Energy Commission was guilty of mismanagement. Now Oppenheimer was drawn into a political battle that showed the reverse side of his sensitive, charming personality. Another Oppenheimer was on view: "Oppenheimer the humiliator, the witherer, the arrogant, impatient condescender of intellects lesser than his own."[5]

Oppenheimer must have been aware that Lewis Strauss, an AEC commissioner, was present in the hearing room. Strauss was strongly opposed to sharing radioisotopes with friendly nations abroad, arguing that such radioisotopes might be used for atomic energy. He had been outvoted on the issue, four to one. When asked to comment on Strauss' concern, Oppenheimer chose words that mocked the commissioner's position:

> No one can force me to say that you cannot use these isotopes for atomic energy. You can use a shovel for atomic energy—in fact, you do. You can use a bottle of beer for atomic energy. In fact, you do.... My own rating of the importance of isotopes in this broad sense is that they are far less important than electronic devices, but far more important than, let us say, vitamins—somewhere in-between."[6]

These words of ridicule brought laughter to the chamber and were recorded verbatim by the court stenographer. It was clear to observers in the room that Oppenheimer was making a fool of someone. Lewis Strauss instantly hated him.

In the late summer of 1949, Truman appointed a special panel of scientists, Robert Oppenheimer among them, to evaluate evidence that Russia had detonated an atomic bomb. On September 23, President Truman broadcast the Soviet success to the world. His announcement set off a chain reaction of its own: demands that the U.S. move quickly to the "next step"—creation of a hydrogen bomb. Ernest Lawrence and Luis Alvarez from the Berkeley Radiation Lab went first to Los Alamos to confer with Edward Teller who had advocated for the development of a thermonuclear, or hydrogen, bomb since 1942. Then they went to Washington. Meanwhile, Lewis Strauss wrote a memo to his fellow AEC commissioners calling for a substantial commitment of talent and money to build a Super bomb.

On October 29, the General Advisory Committee of scientists voted against a United States initiative to build a hydrogen bomb, a decision that pleased Oppenheimer as it was consistent with his personal view. Subsequently, the AEC's five commissioners failed to arrive at a consensus on the question of a crash program to build "the Super" and decided to report individually to the president. Only Lewis Strauss categorically supported proceeding without delay.

In February 1950, the United States learned that Klaus Fuchs had been arrested in London and that he confessed to passing information to the Russians for seven critical years from 1942 to 1949. President Truman sought the advice of a special committee of the National Security Council. The committee recommended that the president clarify his directive "to put energetic development of a hydrogen bomb clearly on record...Truman promulgated the committee's report as official policy."[7]

The fact that the Russians had an atomic bomb had a momentous effect on the political climate of the United States. Anti-Communism was on the rise. On February 9, Joseph R. McCarthy, a senator from Wisconsin, claimed to have a list of more than two hundred members of the Communist Party still working and shaping the policy of the State Department. Although he subsequently revised the number to "eighty-one card carrying Communists," he refused to attach a name to even one of the alleged subversives. Yet the charges were sufficiently explosive to engage the president of the United States in the controversy and to persuade the Senate to order its Foreign Relations Committee to investigate them. Oppenheimer was one of many whose past left-wing associations came under McCarthy's scrutiny.[8]

In May 1950, Sylvia Crouch appeared before the California Committee on Un-American Activities and asserted that Oppenheimer had hosted a secret, elite Communist group in his Berkeley home in the summer of 1941. She said that she and her husband, Paul, a former Communist who was then a paid informant for the Justice Department, had attended this event. In the next few years, Paul Crouch provided damning evidence at many such hearings. In consequence of Mrs. Crouch's allegations, the FBI went to Princeton to interview Oppenheimer, twice within one week. Nine years after the fact, Oppenheimer was asked to establish exactly where he was from late July to early August 1941.

Thus, in the summer of 1952, Robert sought Dorothy McKibbin's help in establishing his whereabouts in that time period. He recalled that in early July 1941 he and Kitty left their 2-month-old son, Peter, in the care of the Haakon Chevaliers in California and went for a few weeks rest at Perro Caliente. The problem for Robert was to establish the dates he was at the ranch, to prove he was there continuously, and that he did not return to California for a meeting. Getting that information required great ingenuity and persistence. His memory of the events was thin. Records that would show proof of his whereabouts were likely to have been discarded. Yet Robert knew that Dorothy would do anything in her power to help him and that she had the contacts and local knowledge needed to build his case. Further, she would be dogged in her pursuit of truth and tireless in the search. And she was. Yellow note pads she kept during June of 1952 attest to her meticulous, detailed investigation and to her discretion as she worked with Joseph Volpe, Oppenheimer's lawyer.[9]

Dorothy learned that Robert and Kitty, along with Frank Oppenheimer and his wife, Jackie, arrived at Katherine Page's ranch on the night of July 11. Kitty and Robert stayed from that Friday until Tuesday after lunch, when they went to their own ranch nearby. Dorothy managed to locate a copy of a prescription filled for Robert at the Capital Pharmacy in Santa Fe on July 14. Dick Kaune, who ran the local grocery store, reviewed his old records and found that the Oppenheimers purchased provisions on July 12, 14, 25, 28, 29, and 30. (It is not entirely clear whether this was Robert and Kitty's private account or a joint account with Frank and Jackie.)

Fellow scientist Hans Bethe and his wife, Rose, visited Robert and Kitty at the ranch near the end of July. Hans noted it was clear to them that the Oppenheimers had been there a long time. Then, in the process of trying to catch a horse for Rose to ride, Robert was kicked in the knee. Kitty took him to Santa Fe for treatment. Dorothy located a receipt for the X-rays taken at St. Vincent Hospital on July 25, 1941.

On July 28, Kitty, driving from Santa Fe to the ranch, had an automobile accident when she met a state truck on a curve, causing head-on damage to the front of her car. Dorothy's sleuthing turned up a receipt for wrecker service, a new radiator, and wheel alignment at the Electric Garage in Pecos, New Mexico, on that date.

Although Dorothy's work did not explicitly prove where Oppenheimer was during the period under question, she demonstrated that it was highly improbable he could have been in Berkeley. In time, the matter was quietly dropped.

In March of 1953, Dorothy received a letter from Robert in which he wrote:

> This is also the hour to put on paper, however, inadequately, a word of the profound gratitude that Kitty and I have for all that you did last summer on our behalf. You can well think that this has played a decisive part in the course of events; and I comfort myself with the reflection that anything done so superbly well must also have brought you a little pleasure....
>
> Our love, Dorothy, I hope we shall see one another very soon.
>
> Robert[10]

When Eisenhower's Republican administration took over the government in January 1953, three changes occurred that directly affected Oppenheimer: (1) the elevation of Republican Joseph R. McCarthy to chairman of the Senate's Investigations Subcommittee; (2) the appointment of Lewis Strauss as special assistant to the president on atomic energy matters; and (3) a new presidential security order. Under this new Eisenhower rule, the measure of a person's fitness for government employment rested not only on his loyalty but on his background and the associations he maintained.

Oppenheimer spent the summer months lecturing in South America. That November, he went to London to deliver the BBC's Reith Lectures—an assignment that he considered one of the most important in his life. When the lectures were over, he and Kitty went to visit friends in Europe, and on the evening of December 7, they had dinner with Haakon Chevalier and his new wife, Carol, at their flat in Paris.

Meanwhile, on November 7, William Liscum Borden, former executive director of the Joint Atomic Energy Committee and then an executive of the Westinghouse Corporation, sent a letter to FBI Director J. Edgar Hoover. Citing information from the government's massive investigative file on Oppenheimer, Borden outlined his deep concern about Oppenheimer's suitability to continue serving his government. Even though the letter contained no evidence that had not been officially recognized (and apparently accepted) for years, it sparked a chain of events that would lead to Oppenheimer's downfall.

On the same day that Borden mailed his letter to Hoover, Herbert Brownell, the attorney general, attacked the Truman administration for promoting a suspected Russian spy in 1946. Now even Eisenhower felt threatened by the activities of McCarthy. In this political climate, he knew the charges against Oppenheimer had to be fully addressed. After consulting with Strauss, Eisenhower ordered a "blank wall" placed between Oppenheimer and the nation's atomic secrets until his case was properly investigated. Even though Oppenheimer's connection with the government and its secrets had all but ended, the AEC ordered a full-scale security proceeding against him. Strauss gave

Oppenheimer the opportunity to resign and go off the government payroll, thus avoiding a full-scale hearing. Oppenheimer chose not to resign.

From April 12 through May 6, 1954, Oppenheimer testified before the AEC Personnel Security Board on his eligibility for security clearance. He was alleged to be a security risk because of his Communist affiliations in the 1930s, including his relationship and final meeting with Jean Tatlock, and he was criticized for his opposition to the hydrogen bomb. The three-member panel voted two-to-one on May 27 not to reinstate Oppenheimer's security clearance. On June 28, the AEC, by a vote of four-to-one, upheld this decision, making clear that, although his loyalty was not in doubt, they regarded Oppenheimer as a security risk. His clearance was revoked three days before it was due to expire.

Dorothy did not attend the 1954 hearing. She was ready to testify but was not summoned. Kitty Oppenheimer was the only woman called as a witness, and she was questioned not on her husband's loyalty but on her own Communist past.

Dorothy was enraged and deeply anguished by the outcome of the trial. She was livid with Edward Teller (whom she had long despised) for what she considered his turncoat statement at the personnel hearing. Early in his testimony, he was asked, "Do you feel that it would endanger the common defense and security to grant clearance to Dr. Oppenheimer?" He replied with a forceful "if": "If it is a question of wisdom and judgment, as demonstrated by actions since 1945, then I would say one would be wiser not to grant clearance."[11]

After Teller was excused from the witness chair, he paused before Oppenheimer, held out his hand and said, "I'm sorry." "After what you've just said," Robert responded, "I don't know what you mean."[12]

Teller's testimony was a serious blow to Oppenheimer's case, but it also inflicted harm on Teller himself. His words created a tremendous sense of outrage among his fellow scientists. The majority of witnesses, including distinguished past and present colleagues in science and government, had testified unequivocally as to Oppenheimer's loyalty and his positive role as an adviser. When Teller came back to Los Alamos after the hearing, he received a chilly reception. In front of his friends and colleagues, Dorothy fearlessly walked up to him and said, "Edward, why did you say what you did?" She was the only one in that whole group who was bold enough to confront him.[13] Teller, for once, had nothing to say.

Nearly thirty years later in a television interview, Dorothy was asked to compare the egos of Oppenheimer and Teller. She noted that there was no link whatsoever in their points of view. Rather she insisted on contrasting their basic characters, using the example of the difference between an orchid (Robert) and a dandelion (Edward). An orchid she explained is "more finely designed and built and delicate and subtle and aromatic" while a dandelion is "something you kick up with your heel if you think it is going to take over your grass."[14]

A few days after the trial ended, I.I. Rabi, Robert's devoted colleague at Los Alamos and Dorothy's dear friend, called her. Rabi was leaving New York for the West Coast and asked her to meet him at Lamy. Rabi knew what her feelings would be after the verdict against Robert, and he wanted to tell her personally what had transpired. They went to the Pink Garter, a dining place near the Lamy railroad station, to talk.

Rabi described the hearing room as a place of no dignity or presence and told how Robert could not get the lawyers he wanted to defend him. He talked of the scientists, including himself, who testified for Robert, and he said, "They paid no attention to my testimony; they paid no attention to any of us who knew him best." Rabi painted a picture of Teller on the stand as someone cringing and ingratiating at one and the same time, rubbing his hands as if unconsciously washing them of guilt and ingratitude. The physical tricks were harder to stomach than what he had to say.[15]

Rabi spoke of Oppenheimer's passiveness at the trial. Why did Robert, who had so often come through comparable ordeals with banners flying, permit himself to be the lamb led to the slaughter? It is a puzzle that those who knew him best could not solve. "If Robert had defended himself, "Rabi told Dorothy, "he would have walked from this trial exonerated. The climate of Washington was for him, and he didn't take advantage of it."[16]

Not long after this meeting, Robert called Dorothy from Princeton. He, too, was heading for California. On the way he wanted to stop overnight at her house for a visit. He did not plan to go up to Los Alamos on this occasion. She met him in Lamy, and they drove in the glow of the sunset to her house. He looked the same, tall and thin, wearing his porkpie hat as usual.

As they had in the old days, he made the perfect martinis, and they sat outdoors on her patio, facing the Sangre de Cristos, rose-red in the sinking sun. The trial was not mentioned. They talked of old friends, and when the sun had set, they went into the kitchen where she prepared the salad and he broiled the steaks. She had planned all of his favorite foods. The baked potatoes were ready in the oven; the asparagus had only to be steamed. They ate, still talking of family and friends. They laughed while remembering one of her visits to Princeton when she found Toni, Robert's little daughter, serving chocolate milk to her pony out of a fine French porcelain teacup.[17]

After dinner that night in Santa Fe, Robert built a fire in the kiva fireplace. Dorothy said to him, "Would you like to talk about it?" His answer, "Yes, I would. Very much." Her first question was, "Why didn't you fight?" "I knew it was rigged," he said, adding, "I simply decided to answer their questions as politely as I could."[18]

Dorothy told him how she had wanted to be there but was not asked to appear. "I would have kept asking the question, 'Why don't you judge him by his performance? Why don't you judge him by his performance? and I would have kept on saying it until they threw me out." And she asked, "Why were no women called?"—except his wife, Kitty. His answer was simply, "Kitty was wonderful."[19]

They talked until three in the morning. She learned nothing more about his reason for passive acceptance of his ordeal. The next day she drove him to Lamy, and he continued on his way to California.

It is a great mystery as to why a man of such intellectual brilliance, personal magnetism, and extraordinary persuasive power failed to defend himself successfully. Many years later, Dorothy said that Robert "was naive in politics. If he hadn't been, his career would have been quite different."[20]

In the years that followed what Dorothy called "the purge," Oppenheimer conducted himself with dignity and the absence of bitterness. With his re-election as director of the Institute of Advanced Studies at Princeton in October 1954, the FBI withdrew its full-time surveillance. In the ensuing years, Robert became a "much-travelled and much-visited celebrity, almost, it seems, a landmark on the map of intellectual tourism; a person whom everyone wanted to meet and to have spoken with."[21] And in those years Dorothy's house and her great affection continued to be a "haven of warmth and renewal" for him.[22]

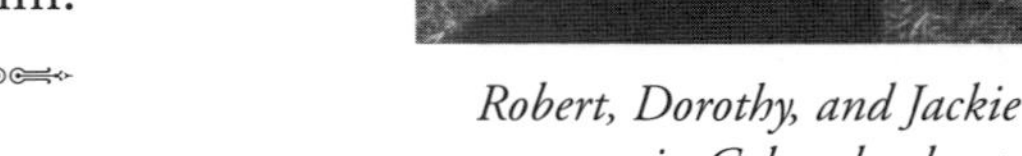

Los Alamos Historical Society

Robert, Dorothy, and Jackie Oppenheimer in Colorado about 1960

Chapter 17

LIFE AFTER GATEKEEPING

Two events of special note marked the waning years of Dorothy's distinguished career at 109 East Palace Avenue: the visit of Queen Frederika of Greece, who came to Los Alamos with her teen-age daughter Sophia in November 1958, and President John Kennedy's tour of the laboratory on December 7, 1962.

Dorothy, along with U.S. Senator Clinton Anderson and his wife, was among the dignitaries who greeted the Greek royal party. The senator noted that "the 41-year-old queen impressed Los Alamos scientists with her knowledge of nuclear physics and showed a sharp sense of humor."[1] While the queen was shown the reactors and other scientific installations and was entertained at lunch by the laboratory director, Norris Bradbury, Dorothy escorted Princess Sophia on a shopping trip into Santa Fe.

En route, they stopped at the San Ildefonso Pueblo. The Indians were prepared for what appeared to be a spontaneous visit because many of the women had been on the Hill to assist the Bradburys with their luncheon and knew that young Sophia had other plans. Indian women wearing colorful ceremonial costumes greeted the princess. Popovi Da, the son of the famed master potter, Maria Martinez, gave

Sophia a book about his mother and introduced her to the famed craftswoman.

Shopping in Santa Fe under the portal of the Palace of the Governors, the young princess bought at least one piece of jewelry from each Indian. Dorothy helped Sophia select blue jeans, cowboy boots, and western belts for herself and her sister. A lady-in-waiting was along to carry the royal purse and parcels.

Dorothy did not have an official role in Kennedy's whirlwind visit to Santa Fe, Los Alamos, and Albuquerque, but she was overjoyed to be a part of the excitement. Along with Joe McKibbin and Robert Oppenheimer, Kennedy was one of her heroes. The whole town of Los Alamos and its neighbors in the valley and pueblos gathered at the Los Alamos High School football field to see the president. In his remarks that day Kennedy paid tribute to them.

> There is no group of people in this country whose record over the last twenty years has been more pre-eminent in the service of their country than all of you here in this small community in New Mexico.
>
> We want to express our thanks to you. It is not merely what was done during the days of the second war, but what has been done since then, not only in developing weapons of destruction which, by irony of fate, help maintain the peace and freedom but also in medicine and space and all other related fields which can mean so much to mankind if we can maintain the peace and protect our freedom.
>
> So you here in this mountain town make a direct contribution not only to the freedom of this country, but to those thousands of miles away. Therefore, I am proud, as President of the United States, to come here today and express our thanks for you.[2]

On June 28, 1963, the Santa Fe office of the Los Alamos Scientific Laboratory at 109 East Palace Avenue closed with little more fanfare than had attended its opening twenty years before. A brief ceremony was held at the end of the workday. Norris Bradbury presented a plaque commemorating the location to the mayor of Santa Fe. He also commended Dorothy's twenty years of service at a gathering of dignitaries from the Hill, officials from Santa Fe, her friends and family.

The closing of the office coincided with the retirement of Dorothy McKibbin and marked the end of an era in which she had been the link between the outside world and the world of research and development at Los Alamos. Dorothy and 109 were synonymous. She was the guiding spirit who set the tone for the warm welcome accorded every person who came through the now famous portal: great men of science, maids, military officials, and civilians from all walks of life. Each was important to the mission. Each was treated with the same respect by the "front man" for the atomic bomb.

Another significant change related to the Los Alamos project occurred just before 109 was closed. With the election of John F. Kennedy, a number of liberal intellectuals who had championed Robert Oppenheimer came to work in Washington. They made a concerted effort to exonerate him publicly. President Kennedy invited him to a White House dinner for Nobel Prize winners. In April 1963, Oppenheimer learned that he would receive the highest honor given by the Atomic Energy Commission, the Enrico Fermi Prize.

The award ceremony was to take place at the White House on December 2. Robert and Kitty invited Dorothy to join them there for that celebration. She planned to attend, but when Kennedy was killed on November 22, she didn't have the heart to make the trip. President Lyndon Johnson awarded the prize to Oppenheimer, twenty-one years to the day after Fermi had achieved the first self-sustained, controlled nuclear chain reaction in Chicago. Johnson gave a brief speech in which he said, "One of President Kennedy's most important acts was to sign this award." Then he presented Oppenheimer with the citation, the medal, and a check for $50,000, "on behalf of the people of the United States." For a few moments Robert stood silently and then he said, "I think it is just possible, Mr. President, that it has taken some charity

Los Alamos National Laboratory

Laboratory Director Norris Bradbury and Dorothy admired the plaque unveiled at 109 East Palace Avenue the day she retired and her office closed.

and some courage for you to make this award today."[3]

Robert later called Dorothy and told her that after the ceremony, at Jacqueline Kennedy's request, Johnson had taken him to the family quarters to meet her. She was still in residence, packing the Kennedy effects, but had not felt up to attending the ceremony that would have meant so much to her late husband...and did mean so much to Dorothy.[4]

Early in 1966, Oppenheimer was diagnosed with throat cancer. He endured surgery and subsequent radiation treatment, but soon it was apparent that there was no hope of remission. His clarity of mind was unchanged; he enjoyed visits with old friends in the short time remaining and spoke weekly with Dorothy. Another era in her life ended on the night of February 18, 1967, when Robert died at home in Princeton. Although Dorothy's unpublished manuscript contains a detailed description of the memorial service for Oppenheimer at Alexander

Hall on the Princeton campus, there is no mention of her attending the service in a place that played such an important part in the lives of the two men she loved so deeply, Joe McKibbin and Robert Oppenheimer.

Over the next seventeen years, Dorothy McKibbin continued to be a leader in the cultural and social life of Santa Fe, hostess to innumerable celebrations in her home, and guest at gatherings of old friends in the Pojoaque valley and in Santa Fe. She was involved in the boards of the Indian Arts Fund, the Spanish Colonial Arts Society, the Folk Art Museum, and the Santa Fe Opera. She was also active in the Museum of New Mexico Foundation and the School of American Research. Other interests included memberships in the Wheelwright Museum, the Old Santa Fe Association, St. John's College Library Association, the Santa Fe Council on International Relations, and the Santa Fe Maternal and Child Health Association.

Dorothy McKibbin Hall, the traveling exhibits room at the Los Alamos Historical Museum, is a tribute to her place in history there. The entrance to that display room is the actual outer gate to her 109 East Palace office.

Dorothy returned to her love of world travel. Among the places she visited in the 1960s and early 1970s were the Yucatan and Mexico, England, Italy, and Greece, usually with groups of friends from the Santa Fe area.

Kevin and his family continued to be at the center of Dorothy's life. Her granddaughters, Anne, born in 1959, and Karen, born in 1962, adored their "GramMac." She visited them at sites around the country where Kevin served as a National Park Service ranger. In a conversation in 2000, Karen described GramMac with a rush of warm feeling:

> She was awesome. She was a real grandmother. She was always interested in us and what we were doing. There was an energy about her that attracted people. She was very comfortable with herself. I

> never saw her as afraid of anything even when she was getting older. I remember asking her about dying. 'Are you afraid of dying?' She said, 'No. I've had a long life and when my time comes I will be ready to go.' But she never had any angst about her, any fearfulness. It was all openness, and I never saw her frightened.[5]

Failing eyesight plagued the closing years of Dorothy's life. After the two cataract operations in the early 1950s, she managed well for nearly twenty years until glaucoma took over. In the fall of 1974, Dorothy stayed with Anne and Karen in Pea Ridge, Arkansas, while Kevin and Mary Gower attended a conference in New Orleans. Kevin rented a car for Dorothy to use to drive the girls to the school bus stop and on various outings for the week they were away. When they returned, Anne said to her father, "Don't ever do that again. Don't leave GramMac here to drive us some place because she can't see." Kevin realized then that Dorothy's driving days were over. He knew how much his mother prized her independence and loved to drive. Taking her car keys away was very painful for him. Kevin's suggestion that Dorothy give her car to Anne (who was just learning to drive) eased the hurt a bit. Dorothy was pleased with that idea. Kevin noted, "If she could give something to these guys, she was always there and loved to do that. And so that worked out all right."[6]

When old friends and family gather to tell anecdotes about her life, dog stories predominate. Dorothy had marvelous poodles who rode around with her. She took them to parties and on trips with her friends. "Cloudy," a big beautiful gray poodle, was one of her favorites. "Never," a Lhasa apso, was her "guardian" when she could barely see. "Never," an unusual name for a dog, came from Dorothy's determination at one time never to have another dog. But she clearly did! Each day she would walk Never from her house to the Folk Art Museum, about a one-mile round trip. Never would run around her legs, causing near heart failure in friends who watched this daily ritual. Dorothy was devastated when Never died of old age. The most infamous of her poodles was "Miss Tari" who became known as "Mystery." Friends thought it was a mystery that Dorothy kept this dog, described as "completely psychotic." It had been raised in a kennel and kept in a cage, so it was never housebroken. Once when Dorothy was in the hospital friends kept Mystery for her. The dog, who was deeply attached to Dorothy, got away and tried to find her way home. She was gone in the desert for three days. Dorothy would call from the hospital and ask, "How is Mystery?" The reply, "Mystery is just fine." Notices about the lost dog had been posted all around the area. Finally Mystery appeared with some other dogs at a house miles from where she had been staying. Fortunately Dorothy was in the hospital long enough for Mystery to get back into some semblance of her former shape before the two were reunited.

After Dorothy retired, friends began saying to her, "Dorothy, you should write a book about your work and the fascinating people in your life." That idea appealed to her. In addition to her personal memories, she had a vast collection of newspaper articles about World War II, the atomic era, and—of course—Robert Oppenheimer, from which to draw background material. She was a lifelong clipper and saver, putting everything to good use. Friends across the country sent her materials from many newspapers including the *San Francisco Chronicle*, the *New York Times*, the *New York Herald Tribune*, and the *Washington Post*.

By 1978 she had created a ninety-one page manuscript titled "Under a Piñon Tree: Old Santa Fe–New Los Alamos." In a series of short chapters she interspersed the history of Los Alamos with anecdotes from her work at 109 and brief sketches of her personal life. She sent her narrative to a Smith classmate, Margaret Petherbridge Farrar, who was the crossword puzzle editor of the *New York Times*. Dorothy and Margaret had been close friends since college days and called each other "Dink" and "Pif." Pif, who was married to John Farrar of the publishing house, Farrar, Straus & Giroux, passed the manuscript along to Daniel Lang at the *New Yorker.* Lang had met Dorothy in 1948 when he wrote a piece on Los Alamos. In his reply to Mrs. Farrar, he noted that the story could be expanded, that there was a "wealth of material." He realized that Dorothy's failing vision contributed to the difficulty of getting so much material down on paper and suggested that Dorothy find an editor to assist with the writing and an agent to interest a publisher in her project.[7]

In 1980, Dorothy teamed up with Dorothy Bell Hughes who was born in Kansas City, Missouri, in 1904. Hughes earned a journalism degree at the University of Missouri and did graduate work at the University of New Mexico and Columbia University in New York. For most of her life she lived in New Mexico and made her home in Santa Fe. She used the Southwest as background in her mystery novels, three of which were made into films.

On May 19, 1980, Dorothy S. McKibbin and Dorothy B. Hughes signed an agreement with Blanche C. Gregory, a New York City literary agent, for a book, tentatively titled *Under a Piñon Tree: The Story of Los Alamos.* Gregory indicated to the women that Howard Cady, an editor at William Morrow, who had been in the Office of Strategic Services during World War II and was familiar with the background of Los Alamos, was very interested in the book.[8]

The authors prepared an overview statement and a synopsis of nineteen chapters for a book of 150,000 words. In the précis, Dorothy Hughes wrote, "It is the intention of Dorothy McKibbin and myself to bring to the Los Alamos story material which is not at present collected into a book. The story of Los Alamos is unique, the building of the new world, the world of the atom, in a place which in many ways had not yet emerged into the 20th Century."[9]

When the two Dorothy's decided to collaborate on a manuscript, Dorothy McKibbin could not see to write. Dorothy Hughes came to her house and worked in Kevin's bedroom, editing Dorothy's first manuscript and working from her extensive clipping files. The two women expanded the McKibbin manuscript to a lengthy treatise on the history of physics and the story of Los Alamos. Dorothy Hughes did the writing. Close friends wonder if Dorothy McKibbin ever read her collaborator's turgid prose. Blanche Gregory was not able to find a publisher and returned the manuscript to the two women. In February 1985, Dorothy Hughes wrote to Dorothy, encouraging her to show the book to the University of New Mexico Press, where Hughes had some previous connections.[9] By that time Dorothy was in declining health, living at home with the aid of full-time help. Disappointed that the liaison with Hughes and the assistance of Blanche Gregory did not bear fruit, she did not continue to pursue a publisher.

While she was working on her manuscripts, Dorothy was interviewed by several international documentary film companies, including Television Roma, the British Broadcasting Corporation, and Pathé Cinema from Paris. In 1980 she made several cameo appearances in Jon Else's film, *The Day After Trinity: J. Robert Oppenheimer & The Atomic Bomb*. Else used archival footage and commentary from other key figures in Oppenheimer's life and the Manhattan Project— including Frank Oppenheimer, Hans Bethe, Robert Wilson, Stan Ulam and his wife, Francoise, Robert Serber, and Freeman Dyson—to give a haunting portrayal of Oppenheimer's life and an incisive review of the nuclear age that followed Trinity. Else's film was an Academy Award Nominee for the Best Documentary in the year it was released.

Dorothy was also profiled in a video, *Woman Who Kept a Secret*, produced by the Albuquerque Public Television Station KNME in 1982. It was on this tape that she made her comparison of Oppenheimer and Teller, the orchid and the dandelion. Dorothy was charming and witty, even a bit feisty. Her plucky spirit dominated the interview.

In 1984 The Network for the Common Good was founded in Santa Fe. It began a program called "Living Treasures" based on respect

In April 1982 Dorothy posed with her dog for Beti Martinez of the Albuquerque Journal.

for elders as engendered in the pueblos of New Mexico, the Hispanic culture, and in Asian societies. Between 1984 and 1997, more than one hundred remarkable older residents of northern New Mexico were honored with the Living Treasure designation, Dorothy McKibbin among them. A book entitled *Living Treasures: Celebration of the Human Spirit* was published in 1997. In text culled from oral interviews and black and white photographs, one hundred four women and men are profiled. Dorothy is pictured on the cover.

In her foreword to the book, an essay "In Praise of Elders," Mary Lou Cook lists several qualities that the Treasures share in common, all attributes that clearly define Dorothy McKibbin. One of the key elements was modesty. "And they did it all quietly, no fuss, no publicity....The other striking quality in these lives," Cook notes, "is a reverent attentiveness to the world, openness, receptivity, kindness....Wisdom without preaching is the core of this book."[11] In Dorothy's profile, the interviewer writes: "As a combination reception desk, information center and travel bureau, Dorothy's office was a hub of life and emotion....With an exquisite combination of tact, intelligence, loyalty, hospitality, humor and motherly warmth, she served as 'gatekeeper to Los Alamos'."[12]

Dorothy died at home in her sleep on December 17, 1985, five days after her eighty-eighth birthday. Less than a week earlier, she and her dearest friends had gathered at The Compound, her favorite restaurant on Canyon Road in Santa Fe, where she was affectionately known by the staff as the "Atomic Lady." It was a fitting celebration of her vibrant life.

Peggy Pond Church—who had dedicated her highly acclaimed biography, *The House at Otowi Bridge: The Story of Edith Warner and Los Alamos,* to: "Dorothy McKibbin for the sake of the old times and the new"—read this poem at her memorial service:

For D

She yields her hair to the wind;
she yields her face to the sun;
her love, like the evening star,
shines clear for everyone.
Love is a light in her.
Love is a warming fire.
The hungry, the sad, the cold
she heals of their long desire.
Men have gone down to death
wearing her love like a rose,
and the tears that her own heart sheds
only her own heart knows.[1]

The citation for an honorary degree awarded to Dorothy by the College of Santa Fe in 1979 sums up the significance and the essence of her life.

Out of the 1940's came developments in scientific research which changed the course of world history. The center for this was Los Alamos, a community which came alive with people from all over the world who brought with them their brilliance, their vitality, their enthusiasm and their dedication. In the very midst of this tense, top-secret, wartime pandemonium stood a calm, intelligent, efficient and loving woman.

Dorothy Scarritt McKibbin

You dedicated yourself to the personal well-being of the hundreds of human beings who came to participate in this vital center of activity. You became the heartbeat of the operation in ways above and beyond the call of duty. Your energy, courage, wisdom, and warmth were felt by one and all.

And now for nearly half a century you have blessed northern New Mexico with your quiet grace, continuing to give of yourself in countless ways to your adopted communities of Los Alamos and Santa Fe. Your warm human qualities continue to radiate and enrich all who come to know you.

ACKNOWLEDGMENTS

Writing the biography of Dorothy Scarritt McKibbin has been a wonderful adventure, due in large measure to the kindness of each person who helped me reconstruct her life, and to the patient, generous computer support of my son-in-law Dan Morita.

It all began on a 1994 journey to Santa Fe. The trip was organized for Smith College alumnae and led by Shirley Reeser McNally and Margaret (Maggie) Weltmer Phinney. It included a fine tea party at Dorothy's house and a brief description of her life. From that occasion I carried away the idea that she was a "power girl" at Smith and a protégé of Robert Oppenheimer.

Four years later I was searching for a topic for a paper to present to the Monday Afternoon Club, a women's literary group now in its 124th season in Northampton, Massachusetts. The theme for the talk was "Women Who Made a Difference." A new member of the group, struggling to find a unique figure, I was listening to a paper on Rachel Carson when Dorothy boldly came to mind. Since I knew very little about her, I telephoned Shirley who led me to several of Dorothy's friends—Mary Branham, Betty Lilienthal, and Francoise Ulam. They brought others into the circle: Mary Brennan, Priscilla Duffield, David and Frances Hawkins, and Dorothy Walker whose memories and insights came to enrich the story. It was Francoise who suggested that I consider writing a full-length biography of Dorothy, and without her support there would never have been a book.

Dorothy's son, Kevin, his late wife, Mary Gower, and their daughters, Anne and Karen, wholeheartedly embraced this project and gave me access to the McKibbin family archives. My appreciation knows no bounds.

Scarritt relatives, Dudley Groves, Pat Metropolis, and James Scarritt, provided family history and anecdotes that enriched the text.

Molly McMillan did the same for McKibbin family background. Warm thanks to all.

Nanci Young, Smith College archivist, promptly answered every inquiry with enthusiasm. New writing friends and mentors: Kai Bird, John Bowman, Gregg Herken, Priscilla McMillan, Mary Palevsky, and Sharon Snyder generously shared their wise counsel and experience.

Very special thanks to the Publishing Committee of the Los Alamos Historical Society for its faith in this new writer and willingness to publish a "first book." Barbara Storms has been a most patient editor and teacher, and I am greatly in her debt for this splendid education. Many thanks also to Gloria Sharp for her cover design that captures Dorothy's spirit and honors Otto Frisch's drawing.

Over the four years of preparing this manuscript, dear friends and new acquaintances wherever I went listened to the unfolding of this manuscript. Few knew the story of Los Alamos, and none knew about Dorothy. Their excitement sustained my confidence that her story would have a wide audience. They are all treasures.

Loving thanks to my husband, Herb, who created a beautiful writing room for me, read every word of the manuscript, and always provided thoughtful suggestions.

NOTES

Entries frequently cited are identified by the following abbreviations:

LAHS Los Alamos Historical Society

LANL Los Alamos National Laboratory

McKFP McKibbin Family Papers, White Rock, NM

MS 1 Dorothy Scarritt McKibbin, unpublished manuscript, *Under a PiñonTree: Old Santa Fe-New Los Alamos* (Santa Fe, NM, 1970s). McKFP

MS 2 Dorothy Scarritt McKibbin & Dorothy Bell Hughes, unpublished manuscript, *Under a Piñon Tree: The Story of Los Alamos* (Santa Fe, NM 1980s). McKFP

DMcKJ Dorothy McKibbin, unpublished journal "The Book of Kevin McKibbin, 1930-35". McKFP.

SBMD *Standing By and Making Do: Women of Wartime Los Alamos,* Jane S. Wilson and Charlotte Serber, editors. Second Printing (Los Alamos, NM: LAHS, 1988).

PART ONE: EMERGENCE OF THE POWER GIRL

Introduction

1. Dorothy McKibbin, videotape interview in her home with Hal Rhodes. *Woman Who Kept a Secret.* Dale Sonnenberg, editor and producer: (Albuquerque, NM: KNME-TV, 1982), two thirty-minute segments. No transcript available.
2. Interview with Dorothy McKibbin (Santa Fe. NM: Historical Perspectives Educational Films, January 13, 1982), videotape transcript, 4.

Chapter 1: Roots in Kansas City

1. Alice Scarritt Kelley, telephone interview with the author, June 1999.

Chapter 2: Setting Out Into the World

1. *Catalogue of Smith College, Forty-Second Year, 1915-1916* (Northampton, MA: Smith College, 1915), 16.
2. Ibid., 112.

Chapter 3: The McKibbins of St. Paul

1. Joseph Chambers McKibbin, letter to his father, December 21, 1918. McKFP
2. Joseph Chambers McKibbin, letter to his parents, March 28, 1923. McKFP

Chapter 4: Sunmount Sanitarium

1. MS 2, 61.
2. Dorothy Ann Scarritt, poem written at Sunmount Sanitarium (Santa Fe, NM, 1925). McKFP
3. Schuyler Ashley, letter to Dorothy Ann Scarritt, November 22, 1926. McKFP
4. MS 1, 47.
5. Schuyler Ashley, letter to Dorothy Ann Scarritt, December 31, 1926. McKFP

Chapter 5: Marriage and Moving On

1. "Scarritt-McKibbin Nuptials," *The Independent, The Weekly Journal of Kansas City Society* (Kansas City, MO: October 8, 1927).
2. Dorothy McKibbin, poem written to her newborn son (St. Paul, MN: December 14, 1930). McKFP
3. MS 2, 62.
4. Faber, Eberhard. "Joseph Chambers McKibbin, '15" (Princeton, NJ: *Princeton Alumni Weekly,* November 3, 1931).
5. Class of 1915, Princeton University, *Fifty Year Record* (Princeton, NJ: Princeton University Press, 1965), 349.
6. MS 2, 62.
7. DMcKJ, 3.
8. Dorothy McKibbin, poem (St. Paul, MN, 1931). McKFP

PART TWO: RETURN TO SANTA FE

Chapter 6: Creating a New Life

1. MS 1, 7.
2. Arrell Morgan Gibson, *The Santa Fe and Taos Colonies: Ages of the Muses, 1900-1942* (Norman, OK: University of Oklahoma Press, 1983),

182.
3. MS 2, 62.
4. Historic Santa Fe Foundation, *Old Santa Fe Today,* Third Edition (Albuquerque, NM: University of New Mexico Press, 1991), 59.
5. Shelley Armitage, *Bones Incandescent (*Lubbock, TX: Texas Tech University Press, 2001), vix.
6. Lynette Baughman, "The House at Otowi: Tearoom Bridges Gap between War and Peace" (Santa Fe: *New Mexico Magazine,* September 1999), 39.
7. MS 1, 25.
8. DMcKJ, 7.
9. Ibid.
10. MS 2, 63.
11. Ibid.
12. DMcKJ, 11.
13. Ibid., 12.
14. Ibid., 13.
15. Ibid., 16.
16. Mary Brennan, "National Register of Historic Places Inventory-Nomination Form" for the Dorothy S. McKibbin House, Santa Fe, NM., Item 8-4.
17. Ibid., Item 8-2.
18. Kevin McKibbin, interview with the author (White Rock, NM: September 30, 1998), audiotape transcript, 7.
19. Ibid., 5.
20. Ibid., 8.
21. Objectives of the Old Santa Fe Association. Old Santa Fe Association file. Quoted in Beatrice Chauvenet, *John Gaw Meem: Pioneer in Historic Preservation* (Santa Fe, NM: Historic Santa Fe Foundation/ Museum of New Mexico Press, 1985), 21.
22. Emily Otis Barnes, interview with the author (Santa Fe, NM: September 30, 1998), audiotape transcript, 1.
23. Ibid., 2-3.
24. Frances P. Lothrop Hawkins, interview with the author (Boulder, CO: September 17, 1999), audiotape transcript, 5.

Chapter 7: Changing Jobs

1. MS 1, 9.
2. MS 2, 64.
3. Ibid.

Chapter 8: J. Robert Oppenheimer

1. Peter Goodchild, *J. Robert Oppenheimer: Shatterer of Worlds* (New York: Fromm International Publishers, 1985), 11.
2. "Oppenheimer, the 'Father of the Atomic Bomb.' Was a Baffingly Complex Man" (*New York Times*, February 19, 1967).
3. *Robert Oppenheimer: Letters and Recollections*. Alice Kimball S m i t h and Charles Weiner, editors (Cambridge, MA: Harvard University Press, 1980), 214.
4. Ibid., 252.
5. Interview with Dorothy McKibbin (Santa Fe, NM: Historical Perspectives Educational Films, January 13, 1982), videotape transcript, 5.
6. David Hawkins, interview with the author (Boulder, CO: September 17, 1999), audiotape transcript, 5.

PART THREE: GATEKEEPER TO LOS ALAMOS

Chapter 9: Establishing the Manhattan Project

1. Jon Else, *The Day after Trinity: J. Robert Oppenheimer & the Atomic Bomb* (Santa Monica, CA: Pyramid Home Video, 1980), motion picture transcript: statement made by the narrator, 11.
2. Leslie M. Groves, *Now It Can Be Told* (New York: Da Capo Press, 1962), 61.
3. Los Alamos National Laboratory, *Los Alamos 1943-1945: The Beginning of an Era* (LANL, July 1986), 10.
4. Fermor S. and Peggy Pond Church, *When Los Alamos Was a Ranch School,* Second Edition. (LAHS,1998), vii.
5. Ibid., 12.
6. Ibid, 16.
7. Mary Burchill, *Lady of the Canyon: Evelyn Cecil Frey* (Los Alamos: Otowi Crossing Press, Copyright pending), 46.
8. Robert Seidel, *Oppenheimer and His Staff Arrive: The Stakes Were High and Time Was Short* (LANL, 1993) Available from *www.lanl.govt/*

worldview/welcome/history12_oppie-arrives.html.
9. Victor F. Weisskopf, interview with Mario Balibrera, #T-810013, (LANL, 1981), audiotape transcript, 7.
10. MS 2, 77-78.

Chapter 10: 109 East Palace Avenue

1. MS 1, 12.
2. Ibid., 17.
3. Ibid., 22.
4. Ruth Marshak, "Secret City" SBMD, 2.
5. Dorothy McKibbin, "109 East Palace" SBND, 24.
6. Laura Fermi, *Atoms in the Family* (The University of Chicago Press, 1954), 234.
7. Dorothy McKibbin, "109 East Palace" SBMD, 27.

Chapter 11: The Early Days on the Hill

1. MS 2, 69.
2. Ibid., 67.
3. MS 1, 65.
4. Dorothy McKibbin, videotape interview in her home with Hal Rhodes, *Woman Who Kept a Secre*t, 1982. No transcript available.
5. Kevin McKibbin, interview with the author (White Rock, NM, September 30, 1998), audiotape transcript, 2.
6. Ibid.
7. Bernice Brode, *Tales of Los Alamos: Life on the Mesa, 1943-45* . Barbara Storms, editor. (LAHS, 1997), 97.
8. Priscilla Duffield, interview with the author (Los Alamos, NM, September 28, 1998), audiotape transcript, 2.
9. MS 1, 30.
10. Mary Burchill, *Lady of the Canyon: Evelyn Cecil Frey* (Los Alamos: Otowi Crossing Press, Copyright pending), 11.
11. Ibid., 29.
12. Ibid., 34.
13. Ibid., 42.
14. Ibid., 48.

15. MS 1, 31.
16. Ibid.
17. Ibid., 32.
18. Ibid.

Chapter 12: The Los Alamos Community

1. Edith C. Truslow, *Manhattan District History: Nonscientific Aspects of Los Alamos, Project Y, 1942 through 1946* (LAHS, 1997), 101.
2. Robert Jungk, *Brighter Than a Thousand Suns: A Personal History of the Atomic Scientists* (New York: Harcourt Brace Jovanovich, 1958), 118.
3. Truslow, *Manhattan District History,* 60.
4. Bernice Brode, *Tales of Los Alamos,*: Life on the Mesa, 1943-45, Barbara Storms, editor. (LAHS, 1997), 37.
5. Charlotte Serber, "Labor Pains" SBMD, 67.
6. Brode, *Tales of Los Alamos,* 5.
7. Jane S. Wilson, "Not Quite Eden" SBMD, 45.
8. Paul Filipkowski, "Postal Censorship at Los Alamos, 1943-1945" (*LAHS Newsletter,* March 2001), 7-9.
9. Katrina Mason, *Children of Los Alamos: An Oral History of the Town Where the Atomic Age Began* (New York: Twayne Publishers, 1995), 11
10. Jane S. Wilson, "Not Quite Eden," 48.
11. Shirley Barnett, "Operation Los Alamos" SBMD, 92.
12. Ruth Marshak, "Secret City" SBMD, 16.
13. Wilson, *"Not Quite Eden."* 43.
14. Marshak, *"Secret City,"* 4.
15. Brode, *Tales of Los Alamos,* 90.
16. Dorothy Scarritt McKibbin, untitled speech (Los Alamos: November 23, 1959), 2. McKFP
17. MS 1, 24.
18. Truslow, *Manhattan District History,* 99.
19. Victor F. Weisskopf, interview with Mario Balibrera, #T-810013 (Los Alamos, NM: LANL, 1981) audiotape transcript, 8

Chapter 13: Trinity and the End of the War

1. See letter of J. Robert Oppenheimer to General Groves in *Robert*

Oppenheimer: Letters and Recollections, Alice Kimball Smith and Charles Weiner, editors. (Cambridge, MA: Harvard University Press, 1980), 290 and Gregg Herken, *Brotherhood of the Bomb: The Tangled Lives of Robert Oppenheimer, Ernest Lawrence, and Edward Teller* (New York: Henry Holt and Company, 2002), 129.

2. Bernice Brode, *Tales of Los Alamos: Life on the Mesa, 1943-45.* Barbara Storms, editor. (LAHS, 1997) 65.

3. Dorothy McKibbin, videotape interview in her home with Hal Rhodes, *Woman Who Kept a Secret,* 1982. No transcript available.

4. Leslie Groves, *Now It Can be Told,* (New York: Da Capo Press, 1962), 297-8.

5. MS 2, 133.

6. Dorothy Scarritt McKibbin, 1959 untitled speech, 2. McKFP

7. MS 1, 1.

8. MS 2, 134.

9. Groves, 415.

10. MS 2, 135.

11. Philip M. Stern, with the collaboration of Harold P. Green, *The Oppenheimer Case: Security on Trial* (New York: Harper & Row, 1969), 85.

PART FOUR: AFTER THE BOMB

Chapter 14: The Future of Los Alamos

1. MS 2, 111.

2. J. Robert Oppenheimer, acceptance speech for Certificate of Appreciation given to the Los Alamos Scientific Laboratory on behalf of the Army, October 16, 1945 (*Los Alamos Science*, Winter-Spring 1983).

3. Bernice Brode, *Tales of Los Alamos*, 139.

4. Ibid., 142.

Chapter 15: Kevin Leaves Home

1. Kevin McKibbin, interview with the author (White Rock, NM, September 30, 1998), audiotape transcript, 10-11.

2. Ibid.

3. Ibid.

4. Kevin McKibbin, Mary Gower McKibbin, Anne McKibbin, Karen

McKibbin, family interview with the author (White Rock, NM, February 25, 2000), audiotape transcript, 13.
5. Ibid.

Chapter 16: Dorothy and The Oppenheimer Ordeal

1. Philip M. Stern, with the collaboration of Harold P. Green, *The Oppenheimer Case: Security on Trial* (New York: Harper & Row, 1969). 113.
2. J. D. Brown, "The Institute for Advanced Study," in *A Princeton Companion,* Alexander Leitch, editor (Princeton, NJ: Princeton University Press, 1978) Available from *www.princeton.edu.*
3. Peter Goodchild, *J. Robert Oppenheimer: Shatterer of Worlds,* (New York: Fromm International Publishers, 1985), 174.
4. MS 2, 205.
5. Stern, 129, quoting *Investigation into the United States Atomic Energy Project,* by the Joint Committee on Atomic Energy, 1949, 277-315.
6. Ibid., 130-131.
7. Richard Rhodes, *The Making of the Atomic Bomb* (New York: Simon and Schuster, 1986), 770.
8. Goodchild, 205.
9. Dorothy McKibbin, unpaged personal notes on the whereabouts of J. Robert Oppenheimer during the summer of 1941 (Santa Fe, NM: 1952). McKFP
10. J. Robert Oppenheimer, letter to Dorothy McKibbin, March 6, 1953. McKFP
11.Robert Coughlan, "The Tangled Drama and Private Hells of Two Famous Scientists." (New York: *Life*, December 13, 1963), 103.
12. Goodchild, 255.
13. David Hawkins, interview with the author (Boulder, CO: September 17, 1999), audiotape transcript, 5.
14. Dorothy McKibbin, videotape interview in her home with Hal Rhodes, *Woman Who Kept a Secret,* 1982. No transcript available.
15. MS 2, 210.
16. Ibid.
17. Ibid., 211

18. Ibid.
19. Ibid.
20. See note 14.
21. Goodchild, 271.
22. *Robert Oppenheimer: Letters and Recollections*, Alice Kimball Smith and Charles Weiner, editors (Cambridge, MA: Harvard University Press, 1980), 332.

Chapter 17: Life after Gatekeeping

1. Danna Kusianovich, "Queen's Knowledge Impresses Scientists During Tour of Hill" (*Albuquerque Journal*, November 30, 1958).
2. "The President's Visit" (Los Alamos Scientific Laboratory *LASL News*, December 13, 1962), 12.
3. Peter Goodchild, *J. Robert Oppenheimer: Shatterer of Worlds*, (New York: Fromm International Publishers, 1985), 276.
4. MS 2, 216.
5. Kevin McKibbin, Mary Gower McKibbin, Anne McKibbin, Karen McKibbin, family interview with the author (White Rock, NM, February 25, 2000), audiotape transcript, 6-7.
6. Ibid.
7. Daniel Lang, letter to Mrs. John Farrar, May 17, 1978. McKFP
8. Blanche Gregory, letter to Dorothy B. Hughes, May 12, 1980. McKFP
9. Dorothy B. Hughes, overview statement for *Under a Piñon Tree, the Story of Los Alamos*, 1980. McKFP
10.Dorothy B. Hughes, letter to Dorothy McKibbin, February 25, 1985, McKFP
11. Karen Nilsson Brandt and Sharon Niederman, *Living Treasures: Celebration of the Human Spirit*, Ann Mason, editor (Santa Fe, NM: Western Edge Press, 1997), x-xi.
12. Ibid., 110.
13. Peggy Pond Church, unpublished poem, 1932. Courtesy of Kathleen Decker Church, literary executor for Peggy Pond Church.
14. Honorary Degree Citation for Dorothy Scarritt McKibbin, presented at the 30th Annual Commencement, College of Santa Fe, May 13, 1979.

SELECTED BIBLIOGRAPHY

Author's Interviews*

Barnes, Emily Otis. Santa Fe, NM, September 30, 1998.

Brennan, Mary. Santa Fe, NM, September 29, 1998.

Duffield, Priscilla. Los Alamos, NM, September 28, 1998.

Hawkins, David and Frances. Boulder, CO, September 17, 1999.

__________. Boulder, CO, March 1, 2000.

__________. Boulder, CO, June 14, 2001.

Kelley, Alice Scarritt. By telephone, June 10, 1999.

Lilienthal, Betty; Ulam, Francoise; Walker, Dorothy. Santa Fe, NM, September 25, 1998.

McKibbin Family. White Rock, NM, February 26, 2000.

McKibbin, Kevin. White Rock, NM, September 25, 1998.

__________. White Rock, NM, September 30, 1998.

__________. White Rock, NM, March 2, 1999.

McKibbin, Mary Gower. By telephone, December 3, 1999.

Metropolis, Patricia. Tesuque, NM, September 26, 1998.

Scarritt, James. By telephone, December 3, 1998.

**Transcripts, audiotapes, and notes are retained by the author.*

Other Interviews

McKibbin, Dorothy. Taped interview, Edited by Tom McCarthy. Santa Fe, NM: Historical Perspective Educational Films, 1982. Videocassette transcript.

Weisskopf, Victor F. Interview by Mario Balibrera, #T-810013. Los Alamos, NM: Los Alamos National Laboratory, 1981. Audio tape transcript.

Articles and Citations

"Baggage, Babies and the Atom Bomb: The Unique 20 Years of Dorothy McKibbin." Los Alamos: The Los Alamos Scientific Laboratory, *LASL News*, June 28, 1963.

Baughman, Lynnette. "The House at Otowi: Tearoom Bridges Gap between War and Peace." Santa Fe: *New Mexico Magazine,* September 1999.

Brennan, Mary. "National Register of Historic Place Inventory Nomnation Form." for the Dorothy S. McKibbin House, Santa Fe, NM. Filed with the United States Department of the Interior, National Park Service, Washington, DC, 1987.

Brown, J. D. "The Institute for Advanced Study." In *A Princeton Companion,* Alexander Leitch, editor. Princeton, NJ: Princeton University Press, 1978.

Corbett, Peggy. "AEC Office in SF Closes." Santa Fe: *The New Mexican,* June 30, 1963.

Coughlan, Robert. "The Tangled Drama and Private Hells of Two Famous Scientists." *Life*, December 13, 1963.

Faber, Eberhard. "Joseph Chambers McKibbin, '15." Princeton, NJ: *Princeton Alumni Weekly,* November 3, 1931.

Filipkowski, Paul. "Postal Censorship at Los Alamos, 1943 - 1945." Los Alamos, NM: *Los Alamos Historical Society Newsletter*, March 2001.

Hay, Calla. "Santa Feans Attend 60th Class Reunion." Santa Fe, NM: *The New Mexican,* May 30, 1979.

"Honorary Degree Citation for Dorothy Scarritt McKibbin." Presented at the 30th Annual Commencement, College of Santa Fe, Santa Fe, NM, May 13, 1979.

Joint Committee on Atomic Energy. *Investigation into the United States Atomic Energy Project.* Washington, DC: Government Printing Office, 1949, 277-315. Quoted in Philip Stern, The *Oppenheimer Case: Security on Trial.* New York: Harper & Row, 1969, 129.

Jones, Don. "Home Has Genuine Santa Fe Pedigree: History, Hospitality." Santa Fe: *Journal North,* May 26, 1987.

Kusianovich, Danna. "Queen's Knowledge Impresses Scientists During Tour of 'Hill'." *Albuquerque Journal,* November 30, 1958.

McMahon, June. "Dorothy McKibbin Retirement Told." Los Alamos: *The Los Alamos Monitor,* June 27, 1963.

"Mrs. Scarritt Is Dead." *Kansas City Star*, November 3, 1947.

"Oppenheimer, the 'Father of the Atomic Bomb' Was a Baffingly Complex Man." *New York Times*, February 19, 1967.

Pillsbury, Dorothy. "Santa Fe Woman Serves in War and Peace." Boston: *The Christian Science Monitor*, July 14, 1958.

"Scarritt-McKibbin Nuptials." *The Independent, The Weekly Journal of Kansas City Society,* October 1 and 8, 1927.

Seidel, Robert. *Oppenheimer and His Staff Arrive: The Stakes Were High and Time Was Short.* Los Alamos, NM: Los Alamos National Laboratory, 1993. Available from *www.lanl.govt/worldview/welcome/history12_oppie-arrives.html*

"The President's Visit." Los Alamos Scientific Laboratory, *LASL News*, December 13, 1962.

"W. C. Scarritt Is Dead." *Kansas City Star*, February 16, 1938.

Books

Armitage, Shelley. *Bones Incandescent.* Lubbock: Texas Tech University Press, 2001.

Bacher, Robert F. *Robert Oppenheimer, 1904-1967.* Monograph 2. Los Alamos: Los Alamos Historical Society, 1999.

Brandt, Karen Nilsson and Sharon Niederman. *Living Treasures: Celebration of the Human Spirit,* Ann Mason, editor. Santa Fe, NM: Western Edge Press, 1997.

Brode, Bernice. *Tales of Los Alamos: Life on the Mesa, 1943-45.* Barbara Storms, editor. Los Alamos, NM: Los Alamos Historical Society, 1997.

Burchill, Mary D. *Lady of the Canyon: Evelyn Cecil Frey.* Los Alamos, NM: Otowi Crossing Press, [Copyright pending, 2002].

Chauvenet, Beatrice. *John Gaw Meem: Pioneer in Historic Preservation.* Santa Fe, NM: Historic Santa Fe Foundation/Museum of New Mexico Press, 1985.

Church, Fermor S. and Peggy Pond. *When Los Alamos Was a Ranch School.* Second Edition. Los Alamos, NM: Los Alamos Historical Society, 1998.

Church, Peggy Pond. *The House at Otowi Bridge: The Story of Edith Warner and Los Alamos.* Albuquerque, NM: University of New Mexico Press, 1959. Eleventh Paperback Printing, 1993.

Class of 1915, *Princeton University. Fifty Year Record.* Princeton, NJ: Princeton University Press, 1965.

College, Smith. *Catalogue of Smith College, Forty-Second Year, 1915-1916.* Northampton, MA: Smith College, 1915.

Fermi, Laura. *Atoms in the Family.* Chicago: The University of Chicago Press, 1954.

Foundation, Historic Santa Fe. *Old Santa Fe Today.* Third Edition. Albuquerque: University of New Mexico Press, 1991.

Gibson, Arrell Morgan. *The Santa Fe and Taos Colonies: Ages of the Muses, 1900-1942.* Norman, OK: University of Oklahoma Press, 1983.

Goodchild, Peter. *J. Robert Oppenheimer: Shatterer of Worlds.* New York: Fromm International Publishers, 1985.

Groves, Leslie M. *Now It Can Be Told.* New York: Da Capo Press, 1962.

Herken, Gregg. *Brotherhood of the Bomb: The Tangled Lives of Robert Oppenheimer, Ernest Lawrence, and Edward Teller.* New York: Henry Holt and Company, 2002.

Jette, Eleanor. *Inside Box 1663.* Los Alamos, NM: Los Alamos Historical Society, 1977.

Jungk, Robert. *Brighter Than a Thousand Suns: A Personal History of the Atomic Scientists.* Translated by James Cleugh. New York: Harcourt BraceJovanovich, 1958.

Laboratory, Los Alamos National. *Los Alamos 1943-1945: The Beginning of an Era.* Los Alamos, NM: Los Alamos National Laboratory, Reprint Edition, 1986.

LaFarge, Oliver. *Santa Fe: The Autobiography of a Southwestern Town.* Norman, OK: University of Oklahoma Press, 1959.

Mason, Katrina. *Children of Los Alamos: An Oral History of the Town Where the Atomic Age Began.* New York: Twayne Publishers, 1995.

Pearson, Ralph E. *The History of the Scarritt Clan in America.* Middletown, Ohio: Ralph Pearson, 1938. Reprint, Higginson Book Co., Salem, MA.

Rhodes, Richard. *The Making of the Atomic Bomb*. New York: Simon and Schuster, 1986.

Serber, Charlotte and Jane S. Wilson, editors. *Standing By and Making Do: Women of Wartime Los Alamos.* Second Printing. Los Alamos, NM: Los Alamos Historical Society, 1988.

Smith, Alice Kimball and Charles Weiner, Editors. *Robert Oppenheimer: Letters and Recollections.* Cambridge, MA: Harvard University Press, 1980.

Stern, Philip M. with the collaboration of Harold P. Green. *The Oppenheimer Case: Security on Trial.* New York: Harper & Row, 1969.

Truslow, Edith C. *Manhattan District History: Nonscientific Aspects of Los Alamos, Project Y, 1942 through 1946.* Los Alamos, NM: Los Alamos Historical Society, 1997.

Wells, Ruth Dyer. *The Wells Family: Founders of the American Optical Company and Old Sturbridge Village.* Southbridge, MA: Privately printed, 1979.

Letters, Notes, Poems and Speeches

Ashley, Schuyler. Letters to Dorothy Ann Scarritt, November 22, 1926 and December 31, 1926.

Bigelow, Allison McKibbin. "McKibbin Family Notes." St. Paul, MN, 1956.

Church, Peggy Pond. Poem. "For D.,' 1932.

Gregory, Blanche. Letter to Dorothy B. Hughes, May 12, 1980.

Hughes, Dorothy B. Letter to Dorothy McKibbin, February 25,1985.

Lang, Daniel. Letter to Mrs. John Farrar, May 17, 1978.

McKibbin, Joseph Chambers. Letter to his father, December 21,1918

_____Letter to his parents, March 28, 1923.

Oppenheimer, J. Robert. Acceptance speech for Certificate of Appreciation given to the Los Alamos Scientific Laboratory on behalf of the Army, October 16, 1945. *Los Alamos Science* Winter-Spring 1983.

_____. Letter to Dorothy McKibbin, March 6, 1953.

McKibbin, Dorothy. Personal Notes on the New Mexico Whereabouts of J. Robert Oppenheimer during the Summer of 1941, Santa Fe, NM: Summer 1952

_____. Speech, Los Alamos, 1959.

_____. Untitled poem, written to her newborn son, December 14, 1930.

_____. Untitled poem. written during Joe McKibbin's final days, 1931.

Scarritt, Dorothy Ann. Poem, written on "Sunmount Sanitarium, Santa Fe, New Mexico" stationery, 1925.

Unpublished Manuscripts

McKibbin, Dorothy. Personal journal: "The Book of Kevin McKibbin.," 1930-1935.

———. "Under a Piñon Tree: Old Santa Fe-New Los Alamos." Santa Fe, NM. 1970s.

McKibbin, Dorothy and Dorothy Bell Hughes, " Under a Piñon Tree: The Story of Los Alamos." Santa Fe, NM, 1980s.

Videotapes

Else, Jon. *The Day after Trinity, J. Robert Oppenheimer & the Atomic Bomb*. Santa Monica, CA: Pyramid Home Video, 1980.

Sonnenberg, Dale. editor and producer. *Woman Who Kept a Secret.* Interviewer: Hal Rhodes.Albuquerque, NM: KNME-TV, 1982.

INDEX OF NAMES

ABOUT THE AUTHOR

Nancy Cook Steeper was born in Duluth, Minnesota. She spent her childhood in Omaha, Nebraska, and Denver, Colorado and attended the University of Colorado for two years. An English major, Nancy graduated from Smith College in Northampton, Massachusetts. For more than thirty years, she worked as an administrator in admission, career development, and alumnae relations at Smith. Mother of two children, she lives with her husband in western Massachusetts. The biography of Dorothy S. McKibbin is her first book.